21st Century Security Dogs

Our Best Friends

OUR BEST FRIENDS

21st Century Security Dogs

Janice Biniok

ELDORADO INK

Produced by OTTN Publishing, Stockton, New Jersey

636.73
Biniok

Eldorado Ink
PO Box 100097
Pittsburgh, PA 15233
www.eldoradoink.com

CPSIA compliance information: Batch#OBF010112-1. For further information,
contact Eldorado Ink at info@eldoradoink.com.

First printing

1 3 5 7 9 8 6 4 2

Library of Congress Cataloging-in-Publication Data

Biniok, Janice.
 21st century security dogs / by Janice Biniok.
     p. cm. — (Our best friends)
 Includes bibliographical references and index.
 ISBN 978-1-61900-000-1 (hc)
 ISBN 978-1-61900-001-8 (pb)
 ISBN 978-1-61900-002-5 (ebook)
 1. Watchdogs—Juvenile literature. 2. Working dogs—Juvenile literature.
 I. Title. II. Title: Twenty-first century security dogs.
 SF428.8.B56 2012
 636.73—dc23
                              2011044849

Photo credits: FEMA photo: 3 (Jocelyn Augustino), 37 (Adam DuBrowa), 39 and 52 (Marvin Nauman), 51 (Andrea Booher), 72 (Amanda Bicknell); National Archives: 61; © 2011 Photos.com, a division of Getty Images: 16, 93; used under license from Shutterstock.com: 8, 12, 13, 20, 23, 26, 29, 31, 33, 38, 40, 41, 49, 55, 57, 65, 77, 78, 81, 87, 88, 89, 94, 95, 97, 98, 99, 100, 101, 102, cover; Frances A. Miller / Shutterstock.com: 63; courtesy State Farm Insurance Companies (www.arsondog.org): 47; Transportation Security Administration: 66; U.S. Air Force photo: 60 (Daylena Gonzalez), 62 (Nathanael Callon); U.S. Department of Homeland Security: 69; U.S. Drug Enforcement Administration: 44; U.S. Marine Corps photo: 36 (Robert Blankenship), 46 (Geoffrey T. Campbell), 74 (Brandon M. Owen), 83 (Caleb Gomez); U.S. Navy photo: 15 (Preston Keres), 42 (Cayman Santoro), 59 (Jamar X. Perry).

**For information about custom editions, special sales, or premiums,
please contact our special sales department at info@eldoradoink.com.**

TABLE OF CONTENTS

Introduction

GARY KORSGAARD, DVM

The mutually beneficial relationship between humans and animals began long before the dawn of recorded history. Archaeologists believe that humans began to capture and tame wild goats, sheep, and pigs more than 9,000 years ago. These animals were then bred for specific purposes, such as providing humans with a reliable source of food or providing furs and hides that could be used for clothing or the construction of dwellings.

Other animals had been sought for companionship and assistance even earlier. The dog, believed to be the first animal domesticated, began living and working with Stone Age humans in Europe more than 14,000 years ago. Some archaeologists believe that wild dogs and humans were drawn together because both hunted the same prey. By taming and training dogs, humans became more effective hunters. Dogs, meanwhile, enjoyed the social contact with humans and benefited from greater access to food and warm shelter. Dogs soon became beloved pets as well as trusted workers. This can be seen from the many artifacts depicting dogs that have been found at ancient sites in Asia, Europe, North America, and the Middle East.

The earliest domestic cats appeared in the Middle East about 5,000 years ago. Small wild cats were probably first attracted to human settlements because plenty of rodents could be found wherever harvested grain was stored. Cats played a useful role in hunting and killing these pests, and it is likely that grateful humans rewarded them for this assistance. Over time, these small cats gave up some of their aggressive wild behaviors and began living among humans. Cats eventually became so popular in ancient Egypt that they were believed to possess magical powers. Cat statues were placed outside homes to ward off evil spirits, and mummified cats were included in royal tombs to accompany their owners into the afterlife.

Today, few people believe that cats have supernatural powers, but most pet owners feel a magical bond with their pets, whether they are dogs, cats, hamsters, rabbits, horses, or parrots. The lives of pets and their people become inextricably intertwined, providing strong emotional and physical rewards for both humans and animals. People of all ages can benefit from the loving companionship of a pet. Not surprisingly, then, pet ownership is widespread. Recent statistics indicate that about 60 percent of all households in the United States and Canada have at least one pet, while the figure is close to 50 percent of households in the United Kingdom. For millions of people, therefore, pets truly have become their "best friends."

Finding the best animal friend can be a challenge, however. Not only are there many types of domesticated pets, but each has specific needs, characteristics, and personality traits. Even within a category of pets, such as dogs, different breeds will flourish in different surroundings and with different treatment. For example, a German Shepherd may not be the right pet for a person living in a cramped urban apartment; that person might be better off caring for a smaller dog like a Toy Poodle or Shih Tzu, or perhaps a cat. On the other hand, an active person who loves the outdoors may prefer the companion-ship of a Labrador Retriever to that of a small dog or a passive indoor pet like a goldfish or hamster.

The joys of pet ownership come with certain responsibilities. Bringing a pet into your home and your neighborhood obligates you to care for and train the pet properly. For example, a dog must be housebroken, taught to obey your commands, and trained to behave appropriately when he encounters other people or animals. Owners must also be mindful of their pet's particular nutritional and medical needs.

The purpose of the OUR BEST FRIENDS series is to provide a helpful and comprehensive introduction to pet ownership. Each book contains the basic information a prospective pet owner needs in order to choose the right pet for his or her situation and to care for that pet throughout the pet's lifetime. Training, socialization, proper nutrition, potential medical issues, and the legal responsibilities of pet ownership are thoroughly explained and discussed, and an abundance of expert tips and suggestions are offered. Whether it is a hamster, corn snake, guinea pig, or Labrador Retriever, the books in the OUR BEST FRIENDS series provide everything the reader needs to know about how to have a happy, well-adjusted, and well-behaved pet.

Today, highly trained dogs specialize in many different types of security jobs, from personal protection to finding missing people and tracking down the causes of fires. This German Shepherd is being trained to bite an attacker who is wielding a weapon.

CHAPTER ONE

Security Dogs Then and Now

Dogs have earned a reputation as courageous, self-sacrificing, and incomparably loyal creatures. They have endangered themselves and even sacrificed their own lives to protect humans. It would be safe to say that dogs have taken the lead in human protection ever since they were first domesticated about 12,000 years ago because protectiveness is a part of the dog's very nature. The drive to protect is innate to canines, just as curiosity is to a cat. From the smallest to the largest, dogs will always have an inherent desire to please and protect their owners. In a dangerous and uncertain world, this is a very valuable canine trait, as we rely on dogs more than ever to provide the security we need to live safe, happy lives.

WHY DOGS MAKE GOOD PROTECTORS

While dogs provide a good source of physical protection, there are many other ways dogs help to keep people safe. Dogs are highly intelligent creatures with an abundance of natural abilities. Both physical and mental traits contribute to the dog's aptitude as a human guardian, and with adequate training, dogs are capable of some amazing feats in security work.

PHYSICAL ATTRIBUTES: A large, strong dog certainly makes a powerful impression as a protector, but

FAST FACT

While we use masculine pronouns in referring to dogs throughout this book, canines of both genders are equally well suited to security work, provided they have the right physical and mental attributes to succeed in this demanding field.

there is room for dogs of many different types in the profession of canine security. While large size does confer an advantage in addressing physical threats, small size also has its pluses. For example, beagles are small enough to inspect places that would be difficult for larger dogs to negotiate. Some airports employ beagles as drug-sniffing dogs, and the U.S. Department of Agriculture uses them to detect illegal plant and animal products being smuggled across borders. In addition, smaller dogs trained for security work are easier to transport and less expensive to care for than larger dogs.

Size does matter, depending on the particular job a dog must do. But size choices would not even be a factor had it not been for our tinkering with canine genetics through selective breeding. Genetic manipulation has also helped enhance the scent-ing, strength, and speed abilities in some breeds of dog, giving us "super dogs" that can protect us in ways we could never protect ourselves. No human on earth can run faster, jump higher, smell better, or bite harder than a dog bred for physical protection work.

Still, nature provided the raw materials from which all dogs evolved. Were it not for their built-in weapons (fangs and claws), their superior athleticism, and their acute senses, dogs would have difficulty protecting themselves, much less humankind. Even so, having the right "equipment" would not have been enough to turn dogs into the protectors they are today. Dogs had to know how to use their endowments, and they had to be willing to use them on people's behalf. Fortunately, dogs possess just the right mental attributes that allow us to mold, refine, and control their physical gifts.

MENTAL ATTRIBUTES: Dogs have a protector mentality for several reasons: They are territorial, they are pack-oriented, and they are predators. All these characteristics evolved for the sole purpose of survival. A dog's instinct to protect his territory stems from a desire to protect his food source and his right to procreate. In the wild, predators chase off other predators in their territory so that they don't have to compete with them for food. Wild canines, like wolves, may also chase off their own kind to maintain peace in their pack, or they may run off interlopers that threaten their hierarchal status and, therefore, their right to reproduce.

This territorial instinct inspires dogs to bark when a stranger comes to the door. Territorial defensiveness is a great trait for a dog that is entrusted to protect property. Sentry dogs in war zones, and dogs that protect business property or private homes, must have a well-developed territorial instinct to do their jobs well. But protecting property and protecting human lives are two different things. Territorial instinct doesn't motivate dogs to protect their human masters, although that may play a part in it. It is primarily the dog's strong sense of "pack" that motivates him to stand by and guard those he loves.

As distant relatives of the wolf, dogs understand and react to social relationships. They build strong

POPULAR SECURITY DOGS

The most common canine breeds used for security work are also some of the most popular breeds overall, according to the 2010 American Kennel Club (AKC) registration statistics. The following are popularity rankings among the 167 breeds recognized by the AKC:

Breed	AKC Popularity Ranking
Labrador Retriever	#1
German Shepherd	#2
Beagle	#4
Golden Retriever	#5
Boxer	#7
Rottweiler	#11
Doberman Pinscher	#14
Great Dane	#17
Mastiff	#28
Bloodhound	#43
Belgian Malinois	#76

It is part of a dog's nature to protect both his territory and members of his human family. This is one of several traits that make canines uniquely suited to guard duty and security work.

powerful weapon against many different threats to human safety. Dogs have the ability to track down escaped criminals, rout out suspects in hiding, locate illegal drugs, detect bombs, and find accelerant residue in arson cases. None of this would be possible if the dog weren't a predator himself with a penchant for play. The dog's instinct to hunt gives him the desire and the persistence to search and find things that are harmful to us, and his drive to play prompts him to search for threats over and over again, as if he were playing an addictive game instead of working.

DOGS AS PROTECTORS THROUGHOUT HISTORY

The dog's natural traits predestined him to become a human protector from the very beginning of his relationship with humankind. But humans are never quite satisfied with nature; they always feel a need to improve on it. In the dog's case, a large size and a nasty temperament were historically the desired qualities for canine guardians, especially those used for war.

bonds with the members of their "family," regardless of whether those members are canine or human. They also possess a natural desire to protect and preserve their family group. Dogs have rescued humans countless times from harrowing situations, even at great physical risk to themselves. This, above all else, makes the dog an exceptional champion for humans.

Such qualities are great for dogs trained for physical protection, but what about dogs in other types of security work? The dog's nose is a

MOLOSSERS: There is archaeological evidence that war dogs existed in Asia as early as 1600 B.C., and these animals may have been the predecessors of war dogs used by the king of Persia in the fourth century B.C. and, later, by the Romans. By the time of the Roman Empire, war dogs had become monstrous beasts with broad heads, massive bodies, and malicious temperaments. Although purebred dogs did not exist at that time, these dogs fell into a general classification called Molossers.

Molossers were often sent into battle with collars of spikes to intimidate and attack the enemy. Sometimes they wore chain mail, or plated-metal armor, to protect them. These dogs were so good at their brutal jobs that they also provided entertainment for the Romans in the form of blood sports. Molossers often fought lions, bears, and even gladiators in Roman coliseums.

HERDERS AND GUARDIANS:
Protective dogs at that time were not restricted to occupations as canine soldiers and professional fighters. Personal protection was important to the people of the time as well: Many Roman homes were decorated with tile mosaics that warned *Cave Canem*, a Latin phrase that means "Beware of the Dog." Personal protection dogs were not as massive as the giant Molossers, but they most likely shared a genetic link to them, because they possessed some of the same physical and temperamental characteristics.

The Molosser's influence did not stop there. Some types of herding dogs also acquired traits of strength and boldness from these colossal canines. Herding dogs had to be

This tile floor mosaic at the entrance to a Roman home in Pompeii warns visitors to "beware of the dog" (*Cave Canem*). The mosaic was preserved under a layer of ash when the city was destroyed by the eruption of Mount Vesuvius in A.D. 79.

smaller and leaner than their monstrous Molosser cousins to do herding work, but the improved physical prowess they obtained from Molosser genes gave them the ability to herd larger, more difficult livestock, like cattle. These dogs helped to protect their owners' property as well. Many farmers, after selling their livestock in town, would tie their purses around their dogs' necks to avoid being robbed on the way home.

As dog owners became interested in developing and preserving specific physical traits in dogs, the concept of purebred dogs became popular. The first dog breeds were developed in the mid-1800s, and many more were established by the beginning of the 1900s. From the brave, strong

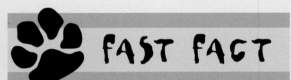

FAST FACT

Historically, dogs that served multiple purposes were the most valued, since it was not practical to own several dogs for different canine jobs. A dog might provide protection, herd livestock, hunt, and eradicate vermin, all in a day's work. Although there are still many multipurpose security dogs, such as police dogs, many modern security jobs for dogs have become so specialized and require so much training that they require single-purpose dogs.

Molossers of the past evolved many of the breeds that protect us today, such as Rottweilers, Boxers, Mastiffs, and Great Danes.

A DANGEROUS WORLD

Recent events have generated a lot of interest in security dogs and what they can do for us. The terrorist attacks on the World Trade Center's Twin Towers in New York and the Pentagon in Washington, D.C. on September 11, 2001, brought the ugly face of terrorism to the forefront of people's minds in the United States. These events also highlighted the valuable work done by our canine partners in security, as search and rescue dogs searched for survivors and human remains in the aftermath of the 9/11 attacks.

Is the world becoming more dangerous? How much do we have to fear? And how much can dogs protect us? There are three major threats that jeopardize people's safety and security in modern times—terrorism, crime, and natural disasters. Regardless of nationality, religion, or socioeconomic status, people all around the world are at risk of being victimized by these same dangers.

TERRORISM: A concrete definition of terrorism is hard to come by, since this term means many things to

A rescue dog is transported out of the debris of the World Trade Center, which was destroyed by a terrorist attack on September 11, 2001. More than 350 dogs worked for over a week to find survivors in the rubble of the twin towers.

different people, but the most common understanding of terrorism includes three components. As its name implies, terrorism involves acts that provoke terror, or fear. Terrorists tend to target nonmilitary (that is, civilian) populations. And nongovernment organizations with political or religious motives—such as al-Qaeda—tend to perpetrate these kinds of attacks. Terrorist attacks may consist of armed attacks, bombings, and/or kidnappings.

According to the 2009 Report of Terrorism, issued by the National Counterterrorism Center, there were about 11,000 terrorist attacks in 83 countries in 2009 alone. They resulted in approximately 58,000 casualties, of which 15,000 were fatalities. The majority of these attacks (60 percent) occurred in Iraq, Afghanistan, and Pakistan. The United States, fortunately, is somewhat buffered from terrorist activity because of its geographic location, but that doesn't mean the United States doesn't take the threat of terrorism seriously.

Shortly after the 9/11 terrorist attacks, President George W. Bush created a new governmental department—the Department of Homeland Security—to coordinate all levels of

There are over 7,000 police canine teams currently employed in the United States.

national security and to help prevent terrorist attacks. This department was designed to strengthen the country's defense against chemical and biological attacks, and breaches of border and transportation security. Subsequently, the U.S. Customs and Border Protection agency began employing quiet heroes—specially trained dogs—to search borders and ports for smuggled chemical weapons.

Terrorist activity in any area may increase or decrease, depending on the political or religious climate at the time. Attacks in the United States continue to remain low, thanks, in part, to tight security measures, the centralized efforts of the Department of Homeland Security, and help from our canine friends. But regardless of how secure Americans may feel, the threat remains, and dogs will always play a major role in containing that threat.

CRIME: It's a scary world—there's no doubt about that. Crime seems to be running rampant and things can only get worse. Or can they? Crime statistics from the 1990s indicate a significant decrease in crime, and statistics from the year 2000 and beyond continue to show modest reductions in crime rates. Those who have studied this decline have explored police, prisons, and social aspects of these

FAST FACT

German Shepherds and Belgian Malinois, the most common breeds trained for police work, can run twice as fast as a human.

crime trends as causes.

One of the chief sources of this decrease in crime may be the effectiveness of law enforcement, according to studies conducted over the past decade. Efforts to maintain order through community policing and addressing low-level crimes appear to have a positive, proactive effect. And, of course, the police dog has been there to assist with this effort.

NATURAL DISASTERS: Although threats like terrorism and crime are human-made problems, there are many threats to human safety that stem from nature's fury. We cannot control nature, any more than we can control the earth's rotation around the sun. Thunderstorms, tornadoes, hurricanes, earthquakes, fires, floods, typhoons, tsunamis, and volcanic eruptions are some of the worst natural disasters that afflict humankind. In many of them, the dog is a valuable tool for locating both survivors and the deceased.

FAST FACT

Although the frequency and intensity of natural disasters continue to climb, disaster preparedness and prevention programs have helped to decrease the number of deaths due to catastrophic natural events. However, the number of people injured, displaced, or left homeless from disasters is still increasing.

According to a disaster database maintained by the Center for Research on Epidemiology of Disasters (CRED) and the Office of U.S. Foreign Disaster Assistance (OFDA), natural disasters have increased significantly in the last four decades. There were 373 natural disasters reported in 2010, as compared to 78 disasters in 1970. Although some of this increase is due to advancements in obtaining and recording data, two-thirds of the increase is due to a surge in hydro-meteorological disasters, such as hurricanes, floods, tsunamis, and droughts.

What's causing all this mayhem on the surface of the earth? There are a number of factors that contribute to the increase in natural disasters. The intensity and frequency of hurricanes have increased as a function of natural cycles; in addition, mass temperature changes in tropical ocean waters, called "El Niño" and "La Niña," are partly to blame. But there are also plenty of human-made causes for the number and severity of natural disasters.

Climate change has a profound effect on weather patterns and appears to increase the intensity of all types of storms. Our meddling with the earth's natural landscape often increases the severity of natural disasters. As more land is covered in cement and asphalt, less water can be absorbed by the soil, which increases the amount of runoff during storms. Deforestation, dams, and other land-altering endeavors ultimately contribute to the devastation wrought by natural disasters. More and more humans continue to populate at-risk areas in flood zones, earthquake-prone areas, and along coasts and rivers, so the consequences of natural disasters continue to rise.

Due to its geography, the United States is subject to many different types of natural disasters, including hurricanes in its coastal and gulf regions, tornadoes in the Midwest, volcanic eruptions as far away as Hawaii and Alaska, fires in its parched Southwest, the flooding of the mighty Mississippi River, and earthquakes along the San Andreas fault in California. No matter what the location or the calamity, dogs contribute their special skills wherever and whenever they are needed.

In 1989, the Federal Emergency Management Agency (FEMA) established the National Urban Search and Rescue Response System, which coordinates the efforts of local emergency response departments (fire and police departments) with search and rescue specialists, including search-dog teams. Thanks to this valuable system, trained search dogs can be deployed to any disaster site in the country.

THE ROLE OF SECURITY DOGS TODAY

Initially, dogs may have been defenders of life and property with a focus on protecting only the members of their human "packs." But today, many dogs work to protect all of us. The police dog makes the streets safer for all citizens. The search and rescue dog helps save any stranger in need. And the military dog protects his entire platoon; in the process, he serves his country.

Selective breeding and specialized training have enhanced the dog's natural talents, creating security dogs that operate with professional accuracy. Police dogs can apprehend dangerous suspects with minimal risk of causing or sustaining serious injury. Military dogs can safely detect bombs. Search and rescue dogs can find victims buried under many feet of rubble with little direction from their handlers.

Security dogs work in all types of conditions, from chilling rains to desert heat. They traverse all kinds of terrain, from city streets and rubble-strewn disaster sites to rocky mountain ledges and muck-filled swamps. They work on their own home turf or across the seas in foreign lands. Regardless of whether a dog serves as a personal guardian for his master or protects society as a whole in a highly skilled capacity, security dogs function with an admirable work ethic. They always put forth their best effort, they are loyal, and they never complain. It's no surprise that many of them are, justifiably, honored as heroes.

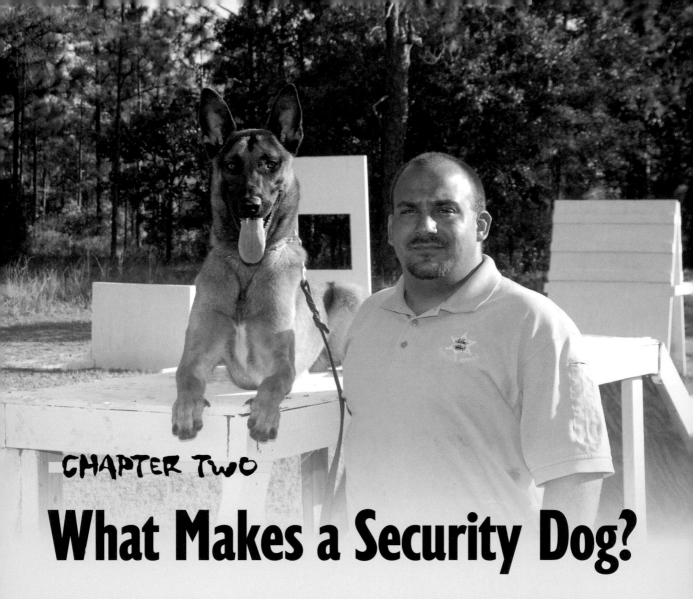

CHAPTER TWO

What Makes a Security Dog?

Every dog has special talents and gifts to offer the world. This was recognized by people thousands of years ago when humans first discovered the dog's usefulness as a protector, hunter, and herder. They found that different types of dogs tended to excel at specific tasks. The selective breeding of dogs for certain physical and temperamental traits became common soon after humans first employed dogs as helpers, because the right traits enabled dogs to perform their jobs with a higher degree of proficiency.

The job specialties of dogs depended on the lifestyle of the community in which they lived. Cattle-

To be effective, a security dog needs a strong prey drive and a high level of courage.

producing areas developed droving dogs that had the tenacity and boldness to drive cattle. Sheep-producing areas preferred gentler herding dogs that would not injure their stock. Boar and bear hunters required large, brave dogs to handle such challenging quarry. Merchants and crop farmers favored smaller, more affordable terriers to exterminate rodents.

When humans migrated, due to the effects of war, drought, or other conditions, their dogs traveled with them. Thus, new canine genes entered local canine gene pools and influenced the population of dogs in their new areas. In this way, new strains of dogs emerged, each known for their specific traits and talents. Today there are many different types of security dogs, from different origins and with slightly different endowments. The following are some of the traits that have made these dogs successful in their jobs.

PHYSICAL TRAITS

Security work can be physically demanding, requiring acute senses, fine coordination, and fast reflexes. While training and exercise can enhance and promote the development of these traits, a security dog needs to be generously endowed with them to begin with. The importance

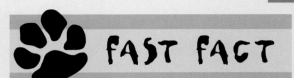

FAST FACT

Security dog breeds are not only some of the most popular breeds in America; they are also some of the most intelligent. According to Stanley Coren's book *The Intelligence of Dogs*, the following security dog breeds are among the top 10 in trainability and intelligence:

> German Shepherd
> Golden Retriever
> Doberman Pinscher
> Labrador Retriever
> Rottweiler

of individual traits depends on the particular security job, but breeds that possess the greatest combination of physical and temperamental traits for security work are favored above others. The more versatile the dog, the greater his value.

SIZE AND STRENGTH: Most forms of security work, whether it is as a canine (K-9) police officer, a family guardian, or a military guard dog, require the dog to be strong and imposing enough to handle threats. A small dog, regardless of his tenacity or viciousness, is simply not capable of felling and holding an adult human suspect. Protection dogs use their weight and momentum to pounce on a suspect and keep him

FAST FACT

Bodily strength is not the only kind of strength required for canine protection work. Protection dogs also need to possess sufficient "bite" strength. This is the amount of pressure the jaws are capable of exerting on whatever is within their grasp. If a dog's bite strength is weak, he will not be able to hold onto a suspect. German Shepherds typically exert a bite force of 200–400 pounds (91–182 kg) per square inch (psi), but with training, German Shepherd police dogs can exert as much as 1,500 psi. A trained Rottweiler police dog can possess a bite strength of up to 2,000 psi. It's obvious why trained police dogs are a powerful force to reckon with.

down, and they use their strength and intimidating presence to hold the suspect until human help arrives.

Size and strength also contribute to a dog's endurance. Dogs used to search for missing persons or to track escaped prisoners need to be able to follow a scent for miles. Dogs with longer legs can cover more ground with a minimum of effort. Although there are security jobs for smaller dogs, the great majority of security jobs go to larger varieties of canines.

FITNESS: Not only must protection dogs be big and strong, but they must also be exceptionally fit. Their jobs require speed, endurance, and the ability to leap over fences or other obstacles in pursuit of suspects. Protection dogs have to have the right conformation and physical balance to meet these demands, and they need plenty of regular exercise to keep their physiques in prime condition.

Dogs employed in security work other than protection also need to maintain their physical fitness. Airport drug-sniffing dogs must be able to tolerate many hours on their paws, and they may have to negotiate tight or difficult-to-navigate spaces. Search and rescue dogs must be nimble enough to explore dangerous and unstable rubble piles without losing their balance. They have to be able to work long, exhausting hours, searching for missing persons in any type of terrain and in any kind of weather conditions. Security work is definitely not for lazy or overweight dogs.

COAT: Security dogs that are required to work outdoors must be able to tolerate challenging weather and climate conditions. Dogs with extremely short hair have little protection from the elements. They cannot withstand extremes of cold for very long, and, despite their light attire, they are not very tolerant of heat, either. This is one of the rea-

sons that Doberman Pinschers and Rottweilers, despite their excellent security qualities, are not as commonly employed in law enforcement and the military as they once were. Police and military dog preferences aside, many shorthaired dogs still find a use for their talents in detection and search and rescue work, since specially made fabric dog coats can help provide the protection their own coats lack.

Longhaired dogs are a little more limited in their potential as security dogs. Although they may fare exceptionally well in cold climates, they can easily become overheated in warmer environments. They also require much more coat maintenance, which is not a desirable quality for a working dog. The best compromise appears to be a dog that has a moderate-length coat with an adequate undercoat for insulation. Thus, the majority of dogs that provide public protection are German Shepherds and breeds that resemble them.

SCENTING ABILITY: Extraordinary scenting ability is a definite plus for many types of security dogs. Police dogs are often cross-trained in drug detection and tracking, in addition to protection work. This makes them more useful and, therefore, more

valuable to the police departments for which they work. Dogs involved in bomb detection, arson detection, search and rescue, airport security, and border security all need to possess outstanding sniffers.

Although all dogs have the ability to detect scents better than humans, some dogs are better at scenting than other dogs. Only the best of the best need apply for a job in canine security. The Bloodhound takes top honors for having the best scenting ability of any breed, so he will always have a role in providing security

Bloodhounds are amazing trackers, but are not well suited for other working dog tasks.

FAST FACT

For many professional security dogs, the dog's handler provides the dog with a home and all the care he needs. When the dog retires, his handler may keep him, or arrange for him to be adopted into a suitable home.

services for humans. Bloodhounds, which were originally developed for boar and deer hunting, are now used almost exclusively for "man-tracking." They are the undisputed experts in locating missing persons and escaped prisoners, but they occasionally help in finding missing pets as well.

Unfortunately, the Bloodhound is a specialist. He is extremely good at one thing, and one thing only. Lacking a protective nature, he cannot handle security work that requires more versatility, such as police dog work or military dog work. For these jobs, humans rely on the next best scenting dogs, such as German Shepherds, Belgian Malinois, and Dutch Shepherds.

Many canine security jobs have multiple requirements for dogs, of which scenting ability is just one. In the case of search and rescue work, dogs may also need to be good family pets, since that is their lifestyle

when they are off-duty. Hunting breeds, like Labrador Retrievers and Golden Retrievers, possess excellent scenting abilities as well as desirable companionship qualities.

TEMPERAMENTAL TRAITS

A dog with the right physical traits and capabilities has all the tools he needs to succeed in security work, but can he learn how to use those tools correctly? Even if he has the intelligence and trainability to refine his natural skills, what will motivate him to perform to the best of his ability? Will he eventually get bored with his job and refuse to work? Dogs are a lot like people in that the quality of work they perform depends on how much they enjoy their jobs. Dogs have natural drives that motivate them and, for security dogs, these drives must be exceptionally strong to keep the dog interested in and focused on his work.

INTELLIGENCE AND TRAINABILITY: Most security dogs need to learn how to use their natural gifts in order to do their jobs. Police dogs have to learn how to take down a suspect, how and where to bite, and how to release a suspect when told to do so. Search and rescue dogs must learn how to follow directions from their handlers when searching a collapsed building or tracking a missing person. Airport security dogs need to know how to alert their handlers when they've detected drugs or other contraband. And all security dogs must have an understanding of basic obedience so their handlers can control them in public.

Intelligence influences how rapidly a dog can learn these things. High intelligence in a dog not only makes the training process go much more easily; it is also an especially valuable trait for security dogs that are required to execute more complicated sequences of behavior, as police dogs do in capturing and subduing suspects. Since canine security jobs require ongoing training to keep the dog's skills in top form, a dog that enjoys using his brain is a definite asset as a candidate for security dog work.

PREY DRIVE: One of the primary drives that motivates dogs is the prey drive. This drive comes from the dog's hunting instinct to pursue things that move. Humans have found many uses for this primitive canine drive, because that's what inspires dogs to chase and herd sheep or cattle. Drawing on their prey drive, most dogs enjoy playing fetch and chasing squirrels. In police dogs and military guard dogs, the

It can cost anywhere from $25,000 to $45,000 to purchase, train, and provide the necessary equipment for one police dog.

prey drive underlies the motivation to pursue fleeing suspects.

All dogs possess some degree of prey drive: This instinct is rooted in canine survival. But many security dogs bring to their work an especially strong prey drive. Oftentimes, security dogs have herding dog backgrounds, and their prey drive contributes to their focus, watchfulness, and desire to search or pursue. Unfortunately, a powerful prey drive can be difficult to control. It's not unusual for dogs with a high prey drive to develop bad habits, like chasing cars or bicycles. It takes a

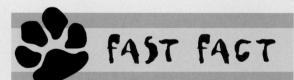

Protective dog breeds, which tend to have independent, strong-willed personalities, require positive training methods. Physically harsh training methods can make them defensive or mean.

considerable amount of training to teach a dog how to control and use his prey drive appropriately.

SCENTING DRIVE: Security dogs that take up a career in scenting, like search and rescue dogs, obviously must have remarkable scenting ability, but they also need a strong desire to use that ability. Dogs that are extremely scent-oriented are highly sensitive and reactive to scents. Although their noses have a very touchy "on" switch, they sometimes lack an "off" switch. Dogs with a strong scenting drive are compelled to follow a scent track to its conclusion.

This powerful obsession with scent gives a search and rescue dog the tenacity to persist until he finds the lost person he is searching for. It gives an airport security dog the motivation to check one more piece of luggage for drugs at the end of the day. Most important, it gives scenting dogs joy in their work, because there's nothing they'd rather do in life than use their noses.

PLAY DRIVE: Security dogs often need to have a strong "play" drive as well, because playtime is a great reward and, therefore, a great motivator for working dogs. A favorite toy to chew, fetch, or tug on is a wonderful incentive for a dog to work hard and do his best. Although some security dogs learn to work for food rewards, food rewards are not appropriate for most, because a

Playful dogs like this Doberman Pinscher may be more motivated to work hard and follow commands when they know that they'll be rewarded with attention from their handlers and play time in return.

working dog could easily consume too many treats for his own good during the course of a day's work.

When using play as an incentive, a dog with a relatively low play drive will eventually become tired of playing and refuse to work. Dogs with a high play drive, on the other hand, have a seemingly endless capacity for play, and they will work almost continuously for play rewards. Just like people, dogs are willing to work harder and longer when the rewards are valuable to them.

ENERGY: Along with their insatiable desire for play, security dogs tend to have an abundance of energy. A working dog that can work tirelessly for hours at a time can accomplish much more than a dog that prefers to lie on a couch all day. A high energy level does more than help the dog to work hard; it also serves as a form of motivation, because dogs that have a lot of energy are always willing to expend it in any way they can. In the case of security dogs, they are more than happy to tap their excess vigor to help people.

PROTECTIVE INSTINCT: For dogs that serve in a protection capacity, a well-developed protective instinct is mandatory. Dogs that show little concern about strangers, or are

FAST FACT

Protective dog breeds, kept as family guardians, tend to benefit from a "hobby" that can keep them mentally and physically fit. Some of these activities include:

Agility
Carting
French ring sport
Herding
Obedience trials
Rally obedience
Schutzhund
Therapy dog work
Tracking
Weight pull competitions
Working dog sport

extremely submissive to everyone they meet, are not good prospects for protection work. Protection dogs need to be willing to defend themselves and their humans.

There is a difference, however, between a dog that's protective and one that's aggressive. Aggressive dogs may engage in uncontrolled and inappropriate behaviors, like snapping or attacking without provocation. They use poor judgment in the exercise of their defensive reactions, which is usually the result of a lack of socialization, mishandling of the dog, or mismanagement of the dog.

Since many security dog breeds are exceptionally popular, there is great variance in the quality of the dogs available for sale. So you need to be sure you're choosing a dog with good-quality physical and temperamental traits.

Protective dogs, on the other hand, are very discriminatory in the use of their potentially lethal force.

A protective dog has a healthy suspicion of strangers (especially those that appear threatening), but this suspicion quickly dissipates when the dog has had a chance to determine a stranger's harmless intentions. Protective dogs may also have a higher than average territorial instinct and a strong self-preservation instinct that will cause them to react defensively rather than submissively if someone attacks or abuses them. When treated well and managed properly, a protective dog will be friendly and outgoing, and have good manners in the company of people and other dogs.

STABLE TEMPERAMENT: A stable temperament is required for all types of security dogs, simply because they work with humans in public settings.

Police departments realize that their police dogs are more than law enforcers; they are also public relations agents. Many police dogs give public demonstrations, visit schools, and greet people on the street. Search and rescue dog handlers know that their dogs often offer comfort to survivors as well as searchers for victims. Security dogs may work in small villages in Iraq as well as crowded airports in the United States. Wherever they are, they have to be able to interact properly with people and other animals.

While genetics plays an important part in how well a dog reacts to those around him, training and socialization also have a positive effect on a dog's temperament. Dogs need to have many positive experiences with people and other animals at a young age in order to learn important social skills. Without such experiences, dogs with a protective nature, in particular, do not have the opportunity to develop the good judgment that allows them to distinguish between threatening and non-threatening encounters. They may very well view all strangers as threats and react to people in inappropriately aggressive ways. They may be distrustful of other dogs and respond to them aggressively as well. These types of behaviors would make a dog unmanageable and untrustworthy for public work.

Socialization has another positive impact on dogs. In the process of introducing a dog to many new people, animals, and situations, the dog learns how to cope with new things. Being able to adapt to new situations is extremely important for security dogs, because they would not be able to do their jobs if new environments or unfamiliar working conditions made them uncomfortable.

The dog training community recognizes the effect of both nature and nurture on a dog's temperament and suitability for security work. Dogs in protective security work always go through an evaluation to make sure they have the right temperament for the job. Training programs for law enforcement, military, or personal protection dogs will not accept dogs that are overly aggressive, excessively timid, or otherwise mentally unstable.

BOLDNESS AND INDEPENDENCE: Other personality traits that help security dogs perform their jobs are boldness and independence. Fearful or timid dogs are not likely to come out of their shells long enough to

Dogs used for police work must have an even temperament and good social skills.

accomplish the tasks required of a security dog. Timidity can contribute to fear-based aggression, and it can also prevent a dog from adapting to new situations. A dog that is bold enough to explore new environments with curiosity and enthusiasm is much more versatile in security dog professions.

Boldness is especially important for protection dogs, because they must have the courage to face any kind of threat, regardless of how frightening it may be. In addition to boldness, such dogs often possess plenty of determination and persistence as well. A well-trained protection dog knows what he needs to do and is willing to do whatever it takes to get the job done.

Protective breeds of dog also tend to possess a fair amount of independence. They are somewhat self-serving creatures that like to do things their own way. While some people consider this trait to be a form of stubbornness, it is a very valuable trait for a dog that may have to use his own judgment in a life-or-death situation. Such a dog cannot always rely on his handler to instruct him every step of the way. He needs to be able to use his own mind and trust his own judgment.

Independent-minded dogs have a reputation as being hard to train, but this is not an accurate assessment. It would not be possible to train police dogs to do their complicated and demanding jobs if this were true. Ironically, independence in dogs is closely related to extreme loyalty and a strong sense of social hierarchy. That is, dogs that are independent are powerfully motivated to please those whom they respect. When such a dog is hard to train, it is usually because his owner is not assertive enough to be respect-worthy.

BREEDS THAT PROTECT US

Not surprisingly, many of the dog breeds favored for security work are also very popular as pets. This confirms that many security dog breeds offer a lot of versatility. Even so, it is always important to consider the "whole" dog when choosing a dog as a working partner or a personal guardian. Each breed sports a unique combination of traits that suit dogs of that breed to a particular type of lifestyle. The following breeds are the most common types of dogs used for security work.

BEAGLE: The Beagle is a handy little dog that has built a grand reputation for himself as both a hunter and a family companion. His ancestors were probably a mix of two different types of English hunting hounds—

Harriers and Southern Hounds. In fact, Beagles were once called "Little Harriers." Bred down in size, the Beagle had plenty of appeal as an economical and portable hunter that specialized in tracking down small game, like rabbits and squirrels. There are two sizes of Beagles today. The larger one is 15 inches (38 cm) high at the shoulders; the smaller one is 13 inches (33 cm) high.

The English hounds from which the Beagle descended were bred to have amiable personalities that allowed them to interact well with each other when hunting in packs. With social structure having less importance for this breed, the Beagle tends to get along with everyone and responds to family members equally. He is exceptionally good with children. Although his short coat and small size make him an ideal prospect for a house pet, he still retains the distinctive baying voice of a hound. He is an active dog that requires plenty of exercise and needs to be kept on a leash or in a fenced area to prevent him from running off in pursuit of wild animals.

The Beagle's hardworking nose and hunting instinct are put to good use detecting drugs and illegal foodstuffs at airports, shipping ports, and customs warehouses. With his wonderful temperament, the Beagle is a

A Beagle's sensitive nose makes this dog very effective at sniffing out drugs, bomb components, and other illicit materials.

natural for working in public places, plus he's easy to train and handle.

BELGIAN MALINOIS: The Belgian Malinois is one of several distinct varieties of shepherd dog from Belgium. Although all the Belgian Shepherds, which include the Tervuren, the Groenendael, and the Laekenois, possess the same desirable traits for security work, the Malinois is preferred for its shorter, easy-care coat. The Malinois is an athletic, medium-sized dog with a brown coat and a black muzzle and ears.

The Malinois's temperament is similar to that of the German Shepherd, with plenty of drive and energy, but the Malinois's size provides some advantages over the larger German Shepherd. The Malinois is favored in military occupations that require the dog to rappel or parachute with its handler. Some police departments and government security departments prefer the smaller Malinois as well.

Belgian Malinois currently find employment as police dogs, personal protection dogs, military dogs, and sporting dogs. They have a great aptitude for agility, tracking, and protection sports like Schutzhund and French ring sport. As their name indicates (*malinois* is a French word meaning shorthaired sheepdog), they also have a natural talent for herding.

BLOODHOUND: The Bloodhound is one of the oldest of the hound breeds, having roots that go as far back as A.D. 1000. This breed has the reputation of being the king of all scenting dogs, especially when it comes to tracking humans. Its distinctive wrinkled face, droopy lips, and long, pendulous ears make this breed easy to recognize. The Bloodhound comes in three different colors: black and tan, liver and tan, and red. A very large dog, the Bloodhound runs between 80 and well over 100 pounds (36–45 kg).

The Bloodhound has one purpose in life—to follow a scent trail. He can follow a days-old track for hours, or even days, on end. His narrow focus and obsession with tracking make him superior at his chosen occupation, but it also presents challenges in managing this dog as a pet. The Bloodhound's determination on the trail translates into a very stubborn, willful nature, which can provide challenges in training.

The Bloodhound today is the "top dog" when it comes to man-tracking, whether searching for missing persons or hunting down escaped prisoners. The breed has earned so much respect in its field that courts of law accept the results of a Bloodhound's trailing endeavors as evidence in criminal trials. Police departments, corrections departments, and other government units currently rely on Bloodhounds.

BOXER: The compact and powerful Boxer came from fighting dogs of Molosser descent, and the breed was further developed in Germany in the 1800s. Its most distinctive feature is its short muzzle. The Boxer's tail is customarily docked, and its ears may be cropped or left natural. This breed comes in different shades and patterns of fawn and brindle. The Boxer's medium size and short coat make him exceptionally clean and easy to care for, which explains why he has become such a popular house pet.

The breed's temperament also makes him well-suited to family life: He is affectionate and loyal to family members, and he is excellent with children. Add these qualities to the Boxer's alertness and protective nature, and it's clear why this breed continues to increase in popularity as a family guardian. The Boxer is an excellent watchdog and guard dog.

Although Boxers occasionally find employment as police dogs, and as couriers and guard dogs in the military, they are most popular as family guardians. The versatility of the Boxer is evident in the breed's many occupations and hobbies, including

agility, Schutzhund, therapy dog work, and service dog work.

DOBERMAN PINSCHER: The Doberman Pinscher is another German breed that has become an outstanding human guardian. Karl Louis Dobermann, a breeder from Apolda, Germany, was the mastermind behind the Doberman's development in the late 1800s. (The final *n* in Dobermann's last name was eventually dropped in the breed name by American fanciers.) He sought to create a larger dog with the same tenacity as a terrier, and he embarked on a breeding program that would eventually produce dogs with an

The Boxer is a muscular, alert dog that takes his duties as protector of his human family and home very seriously.

CHARACTERISTICS OF POPULAR SECURITY DOG BREEDS

Breed	Size	Longevity	Guarding Ability	Watchdog Ability	Scenting Ability
Beagle	20–25 lbs. (9–11 kg)	12–15 yrs.	Low	Medium	High
Belgian Malinois	55–75 lbs. (25–34 kg)	10–12 yrs.	High	High	High
Bloodhound	80–110 lbs. (36–50 kg)	10–12 yrs.	Low	Low	High
Boxer	55–70 lbs. (25–32 kg)	11–14 yrs.	High	High	Medium
Doberman Pinscher	60–85 lbs. (27–39 kg)	11–13 yrs.	High	High	High
Dutch Shepherd	65–75 lbs. (30–34 kg)	12–14 yrs.	High	High	High
German Shepherd	60–110 lbs. (27–50 kg)	10–12 yrs.	High	High	High
Golden Retriever	55–75 lbs. (25–34 kg)	10–12 yrs.	Low	Medium	High
Great Dane	100–160 lbs. (45–73 kg)	7–10 yrs.	High	Low	Medium
Labrador Retriever	55–75 lbs. (25–34 kg)	10–12 yrs.	Low	Medium	High
Mastiff	150–250 lbs. (68–114 kg)	7–9 yrs.	High	Low	Medium
Rottweiler	85–120 lbs. (39–54 kg)	10–12 yrs.	High	High	High

amazingly athletic build, a protective nature, and exceptional boldness.

Since an intimidating appearance was important for a protection dog, it became customary to crop the Doberman's ears. The Doberman's tail was also docked, a practice that may have been inspired when some early Dobermans were born with naturally bobbed tails. The Doberman Pinscher quickly gained the respect and admiration of other dog fanciers, including Otto Goeller, who continued to refine the breed after Karl Louis Dobermann's death in 1894.

Modern Dobermans are sleek and powerful canines—agile, intelligent, and courageous. Like many other protective breeds, they are independent-minded and extremely loyal. These qualities made the Doberman exceptionally well-suited to military work in Germany during World War I. The breed subsequently became the dog of choice for the U.S. Marines during World War II, where they were employed as sentinels, guards, and messengers. Today, they are also used for search and rescue work and therapy dog work, as guide dogs for the blind, and for a number of active dog sports.

True to his reputation for versatility, the Doberman Pinscher is also an excellent candidate for personal protection. Modern Dobermans, quite docile in temperament, are excellent family dogs, and their short, sleek coats make them exceptionally clean house pets. However, they are active dogs that demand plenty of exercise.

DUTCH SHEPHERD: Although the American Kennel Club (AKC) does not recognize the breed, the Dutch Shepherd is becoming increasingly favored as a police dog in America. This is a multitalented herding dog of Dutch origin that has a very strong work ethic. Compared to the typical German Shepherd police dog, it is smaller and leaner, making the Dutch Shepherd more agile and easier to transport or carry when necessary.

The Dutch Shepherd comes in different coat types, including short-haired, longhaired, and wirehaired. The shorthaired variety is preferred as a working dog, since it is easier to maintain. All three varieties come in a brindle color, and most have a black mask over the face.

The breed's high exercise requirements may not make these dogs ideal house pets. Because of the breed's rarity in the United States, it is difficult to find purebred Dutch Shepherds in this country. Many of the Dutch Shepherds employed in police work are imported directly from Europe.

GERMAN SHEPHERD: By far the most common breed for police work and personal protection in the United States is the German Shepherd. The breed's versatility as both a working dog and a family dog has contributed to its widespread popularity. The German Shepherd is intelligent, easy to train, athletic, and has a strong work ethic. German Shepherds' talents in protection and scenting work have made them a jack-of-all-trades in the security field.

Historians credit Max von Stephanitz, whose goal was to create a superior working dog, with the development of the breed in Germany in the late 1800s. The German Shepherd first gained recognition for its working ability during World War I, when Germany employed the breed in its military. German Shepherds were utilized even more extensively in World War II—by both the Axis and the Allies—

The brave, intelligent, and versatile German Shepherd is probably the most popular type of dog used by police forces and the military today.

as guard dogs and sentries. It didn't take long for the rest of the world to notice this breed's amazing abilities.

Today, the German Shepherd works in many capacities—as a police dog, tracking dog, personal protection dog, military dog, search and rescue dog, living assistance dog, a guide dog for the blind, and even a therapy dog. For a loyal companion and devout protector, you can do no better than the German Shepherd. However, the breed's immense popularity contributes to substandard breeding practices, as unscrupulous breeders produce inferior dogs to make a profit. To avoid an unstable temperament and inherited health conditions, it is crucial to choose a well-bred specimen of the breed.

GOLDEN RETRIEVER: The Golden Retriever has its roots in Scotland, where dog fancier Sir Dudley Marjoribanks worked to produce a superior retrieving dog that had a love of water and could retrieve over rough terrain. Marjoribanks's efforts yielded the modern Golden Retriever, which has, as its name suggests, a coat that ranges from a bright gold to a coppery gold in color. This beautiful, flowing coat provides the dog with waterproofing and protection from the elements. Perhaps even more attractive than this dog's exterior wrapping is what's on the inside.

The Golden Retriever has an exceptionally high will to please, is easy to train, and gets along well with children. His splendid temperament and companionship qualities have earned him a place as one of the most popular dogs in America. The Golden Retriever's trainability and hunting drive have also made him a top-notch security dog. Golden Retrievers are frequently tapped for security jobs that benefit from the breed's strong scenting ability, including airport security, border security, search and rescue, and arson investigation. The breed is so versatile that Goldens have found employment as assistance dogs and guide dogs for the blind as well.

Golden Retrievers like "Sandy" are well suited to search and rescue work.

For home security, the Golden Retriever is an especially valuable companion for anyone who lives near a body of water: This breed has a reputation for saving drowning swimmers. Although the breed is not a very good guard dog prospect, since Golden Retrievers tend to view everyone as a friend, they still make good watchdogs.

GREAT DANE: The Great Dane doesn't hail from Denmark—it acquired its surname through some quirk of history—but it definitely lives up to its first name. One of the largest breeds of dog, the Great Dane ranges from 100 pounds to almost 200 pounds (45–91 kg). The breed evolved from the giant Molossers of antiquity and was further developed in Germany as a hunting hound in the late 1700s and early 1800s. Such massive hounds were good for hunting formidable quarry like boar.

When boar hunting diminished in popularity in Europe, the Great Dane made a lucrative living as an elegant and courageous estate dog. To this day, the Great Dane still does a superb job of protecting his humans and their property. His size alone is an effective deterrent to crime, and he is not afraid to use his weight to his advantage, when necessary.

Although the Great Dane is too large to be of practical use as a police dog or military dog, he has many qualities that make him an excellent family and home guardian. With his short coat and clean habits, he's a good indoor pet, and his "gentle giant" temperament is perfect for family life. The only disadvantages to owning a Great Dane are related to the dog's size: Great Danes take up a lot of room and are more expensive to keep than most other breeds.

The Great Dane's size makes these dogs ideal as personal protection dogs.

LABRADOR RETRIEVER: The most popular dog in America, without question, is the Labrador Retriever. Like the Golden Retriever, this versatile hunting breed possesses a lovely companion temperament, intelligence, and trainability. If he has any advantage over the Golden Retriever, it would be his shorter, easy-care coat, which comes in black, yellow, or a chocolate color.

Interestingly, this breed did not start out as a hunting dog. Its lineage goes back to Newfoundland, where fishermen used the dog to retrieve their fishing nets from the water. Dog fanciers in England subsequently developed the breed into the hunting retriever we know today. The breed became one of the most successful field-trial retrievers in the canine world.

Today, Labrador Retrievers are employed wherever their talented noses can be put to good use, such as in arson detection, drug detection, and bomb detection. Their swimming ability is utilized in water rescues, and their intelligence and trainability make them well-suited as service dogs for the handicapped. The amiable Labrador is too friendly to be a guard dog, but he is generally an alert watchdog.

MASTIFF: The Mastiff is the breed that most closely resembles the large Molossers of the past that were used

A Labrador Retriever barks to alert his handler that he has found the scent of human remains in the ruins of this house destroyed by a natural disaster.

as war dogs and fighting dogs as far back as 3,500 years ago. One of the largest breeds in weight, Mastiffs can reach well over 200 pounds (91 kg). This dog is solid bulk, which translates into a lot of physical power. The most common color is fawn with a black mask, but there are also apricot and brindle Mastiffs.

Today's Mastiff is a gentle creature with strong attachments to his family. Although friendly, he has not left behind the protective nature that has defined him for thousands of years. Like the Great Dane, this massive canine became an impressive estate dog, charged with guarding his owner's property.

Although the Mastiff is too large to assist in professional security jobs, like police or military work, he still makes an excellent family guardian. There are not many burglars who are brave enough or foolish enough to tangle with this giant dog. Although the Mastiff's exercise requirements

are modest, he does require sufficient room to move around, and the expenses to keep such a large dog can be significant.

ROTTWEILER: The Rottweiler is a robust breed that originated in the small town of Rottweil, Germany, around A.D. 73. As a cattle drover, the Rottweiler was strong and bold, having acquired some of his physical bulk from Molosser ancestors. His ample physique also suited him as a draft dog and personal protector.

The Rottweiler's size and temperament would be enough to discourage those with nefarious intentions, but

Although the Mastiff has a gentle disposition, its sheer size is often enough to deter a would-be attacker. These dogs are massive, with the typical male weighing 150 to 250 pounds (68 to 114 kg). Female Mastiffs are a little smaller, typically weighing between 120 and 200 pounds (54 and 91 kg).

his black-and-tan coloring no doubt adds to this dog's fearsome image. The Rottweiler's tail is customarily docked at the first or second vertebra, a practice that may have its roots in the dog's history as a working dog. Tails are prone to injury for dogs that work with livestock, and so it became commonplace to amputate the tails of certain types of working dogs when they were only a few days old. This characteristic contributes to the Rottweiler's blocky, well-muscled appearance.

German police associations first recognized the Rottweiler's potential for security work around 1910. The breed also found a niche in military work in Germany during World War I. It took a while for the breed to become established in the United States, but through the 1970s and 1980s, the Rottweiler steadily gained admirers. The breed found opportunities for employment as both police dogs and personal protectors.

Rottweilers are not as common in law enforcement as they once were: More versatile breeds like German Shepherds, Belgian Malinois, and Dutch Shepherds are now favored for police work. However, Rottweilers are still in high demand for personal protection. With his short, easy-care coat, the Rottweiler fits well as house pet, and a well-

The large and powerful Rottweiler makes an intimidating personal protection dog.

bred, well-trained Rottweiler is an excellent family companion.

❧❧❧❧

Many security dog breeds make good all-around working dogs and pets. It is this multipurpose adaptability that has made so many of them popular around the globe. Surely, it says a great deal about the character of these breeds when so many humans choose to own them.

CHAPTER THREE

Types of Security Dog Training

Canine jobs, just like human jobs, have become progressively more specialized over the years. Even though some dogs are cross-trained in more than one security function, there is no one dog that can "do it all." It takes a considerable amount of training to teach a dog how to do just one security task, and although it may be cost-effective to have a police dog that can both apprehend suspects and do drug searches, it may not be worth the investment to also teach him to detect accelerants and bombs.

Focusing on one or two areas of expertise allows a security dog to become very, very good at his job.

One soldier acts as an aggressor while another handles the dog during this training exercise.

Many security dogs participate in intense training and practice sessions to hone and maintain their special skills. The types of training available for security dogs fall into several categories: detection, search and tracking, protection, and sport.

DETECTION

The dog's astounding scenting abilities have been put to good use in a number of security specialties, including drug detection, explosives detection, and accelerant detection. The opportunities in detection work have expanded significantly since the September 11, 2001, terrorist attacks. They will undoubtedly continue to broaden as we learn more about how the dog processes scents and how to use dogs to our best advantage.

The dog's nose may be incredibly powerful, but it takes training before this canine talent can be useful in detection work. In any form of scent detection, the dog needs to learn how to alert his handler when he's found something. Dogs learn to give either an aggressive (or active) alert, which involves scratching or barking at the location of the scent, or a passive alert, which involves sitting down as soon as the dog detects a scent.

The type of alert is generally specific to the type of detection work.

For instance, bomb-detection dogs use only passive alerts, for obvious reasons—scratching or pawing at a bomb could be disastrous. Accelerant-detecting dogs often use passive alerts as well, to keep from destroying evidence. For drug-detecting dogs, however, an active alert may be more effective in locating cleverly hidden illegal drugs.

Reputable training facilities that specialize in detection dog training also incorporate training for the dog handlers, since detection work is a team effort that requires dog handlers to recognize and respond to signals from the dog. Detection dog handlers need to be able to tell when the dog has lost a scent or has to reexamine a questionable target. They need to know how to perform successful searches, and understand the legal ramifications of conducting searches. Performing searches in a thorough

FAST FACT

Dogs can detect odors at 24 parts per million, while humans can only detect odors at 60 parts per million. Parts per million is a measure of the concentration of a substance, which, in this case, is the concentration of scent molecules in the air.

and professional manner provides strong support for court cases that may result from the search.

As with any type of dog training, detection dogs do require ongoing practice to keep them at the top of their game. Accuracy in detection is of primary importance. Canine certification for many types of detection work is available through the National Narcotic Detector Dog Association (NNDDA), which requires recertification testing every year. Most detection dogs receive at least 10 weeks of initial training, although it may take up to a year or more to train a detection dog to recognize a great variety of scents.

DRUG DETECTION: A detection dog will only give his handler an alert for the substances he has learned how to locate. Drug detection dogs will not issue an alert for most prescription drugs or over-the-counter medications. The most common illegal drugs that detection dogs search for include marijuana, heroin, cocaine, and methamphetamines, which is why drug detection dogs are more accurately referred to as "narcotics detection dogs."

Detection dog trainers use the dog's insatiable desire to play to train him and reward him when he makes an accurate find. Training usually begins by teaching the dog to play tug-of-war with a small towel. Then the trainer will begin to roll up a small amount of drugs in the towel. Soon, the dog learns to associate the game of tug-of-war with that scent, and he will seek out anything that smells like that drug.

A U.S. Drug Enforcement Administration (DEA) detection dog, photographed with 209 pounds of cocaine that he discovered during an investigation in California.

Once a dog learns to detect one type of drug, the trainer can then introduce another drug by wrapping it in the towel. Eventually, the dog will learn to associate a number of drug scents with his tug towel, and he'll give an alert to these scents whenever and wherever he finds them. The dog may practice searching vehicles, schools, warehouses, and commercial buildings in the course of his training.

BOMB DETECTION: Bomb detection dogs are actually "explosives detection" dogs, because they don't just search for bombs; they locate all kinds of materials that are used to construct bombs. Some of the components bomb detection dogs target

BOMB COMPONENTS TRAINED DOGS CAN DETECT

Ammonium Nitrate .... A high-nitrate fertilizer, sometimes used as an oxidizing agent in explosive devices, most famously used in the 1995 bombing of a federal office building in Oklahoma City.

Detonation Cord .... A high-speed fuse, used to detonate a bomb.

Dynamite .... A common industrial and military explosive.

Nitro Compounds .... Including Alphatic Nitro, Aromatic Nitro, and Nitromethane compounds, which are explosive organic-chemical compounds.

PETN (Pentaerythritol Tetranitrate) .... A common component of plastic explosives.

RDX (Research Department Explosive) .... An explosive that is often mixed with other types of explosives.

Slurry Gel .... A gel-type explosive consisting of a mixture of various oxidizers or fuels.

TATP (Triacetone Triperoxide) .... A less stable type of explosive, used by terrorists because it is easy to manufacture.

TNT (Trinitrotoluene) .... A common industrial and military explosive.

In combat areas like Iraq and Afghanistan, the U.S. military uses trained dogs to search for improvised explosive devices (IEDs) that could harm soldiers or civilians.

are TNT, dynamite, detonation cord, and many types of explosive chemicals. Since many explosive materials are used in combination with each other, bomb detection dogs must learn how to detect various chemical mixtures of these materials, rather than strictly pure substances.

Trainers at the U.S. Bureau of Alcohol, Tobacco and Firearms (ATF) use food and praise reward conditioning to train their explosives detection dogs to recognize the scents of bomb components. Training a bomb detection dog also involves exposing the dog to real-life scenarios and environments that he will encounter in the course of his job. The dog may receive training in schools, stadiums, shopping centers, and combat zones. Bomb detection dogs always give a passive alert by sitting down near the source of the scent.

ACCELERANT DETECTION:
Accelerant detection dogs help solve arson cases by looking for acceler-

ants, which are the highly flammable substances arsonists use to start fires. Like other types of detection dogs, accelerant detection dogs must have a strong play drive to keep them motivated, and they also need boldness and an even temperament to handle chaotic or crowded fire scenes without getting skittish. In fact, it has become common practice for accelerant detection dog handlers to walk their dogs through the crowds at fire scenes. On a number of occasions, accelerant detection dogs have alerted their trainers to someone in the crowd who had accelerants on his clothing, and the person later turned out to be the arsonist.

Accelerant detection training is conducted in much the same way as narcotics detection training, with the use of a towel or a toy to harbor a scent that the dog can learn to recognize and associate with play. In this case, the trainer puts a single drop of evaporated gasoline in the middle of the towel, rolls it up, and ties up the ends. Trainers use gasoline that is evaporated to 50 percent of its volume because it is similar to the evaporated gasoline residue the dog will find at an arson scene.

After the dog has played with the towel for several training sessions and has become accustomed to the scent in it, his trainer will hide the towel and ask the dog to find it. The dog receives some playtime or a food reward for correct finds. The next step is to teach the dog to give an alert when he finds the towel. A passive "Sit" alert is preferable in accelerant detection, because an aggressive alert may destroy evidence. An aggressive alert may also cause injuries to the dog, as fire scenes are often littered with nails, broken glass, and other hazardous debris that can hurt a dog's paws if he scratches at the site of a scent.

When the dog becomes consistent in detecting evaporated gasoline, his education expands to encompass other types of evaporated accelerants, like kerosene and turpentine.

An arson dog has been trained to sniff out tiny traces of accelerants that could have been used to start a fire. Many arson dogs are Labrador Retrievers like the one pictured here.

The dog may also learn to pinpoint the exact location of a scent by nosing or touching the location with a paw when his trainer commands him to "Show me." The dog's handler can then collect samples from the targeted area for laboratory analysis. Accelerant detection dogs can detect accelerants up to 18 days after a fire.

Accelerant detection dogs also assist in searching vehicles, containers, clothing, and other items for accelerants in the process of tracking down arsonists. Canine accelerant detectors are much more sensitive and accurate than human-made "sniffing" devices, like the hydrocarbon gas detector. However, the dog, as a tool, requires considerable maintenance to keep him functioning at peak performance. Ongoing training for up to an hour a day may be required.

Accelerant detection dogs can receive certification by participating in a training program underwritten by State Farm Insurance and facilitated through Maine Specialty Dogs and the Maine Criminal Justice Academy. This training program consists of five weeks of training for the dog and handler, and an annual three-day recertification training course. The ATF trains and certifies its own dogs, which the agency provides to federal, state, and local authorities in cases that require ATF intervention.

SEARCH AND TRACKING

The dog's nose is an amazing work of nature. Dogs can detect cancer just by smelling someone's breath. They can smell through water and soil. They can detect scents that are days and sometimes weeks old. They can even tell in which direction a person or animal has walked, just by comparing the scents of individual footprints. The dog's remarkable sense of smell has assisted humankind in many different ways, but the most dramatic use of the dog's nose is in search and tracking.

Locating a lost child, rescuing survivors buried in the debris of an earthquake, bringing home the dead to their loved ones, and tracking down dangerous escaped criminals are canine scenting jobs that evoke powerful emotions for everyone involved. Fear, excitement, sorrow, and happiness can bring dog handlers, rescue services personnel, survivors, and victims through some of the highest of highs and the lowest of lows emotionally. But, to the dogs, it's all in a day's work.

MISSING PERSONS: Training a dog to find a missing person is a lot like playing hide-and-seek: It involves sending the dog to find a person who has been hidden. Most dogs love this game, especially when they receive rewards for their finds. Dogs that have an intense interest in searching and tracking get even more enjoyment out of it.

FAST FACT

Successful scent tracking depends on more than the dog's nose. Tracking dog handlers have to learn how to "read" their dogs accurately. This involves paying attention to the signals their dogs give, so they can tell when the dog has lost a scent or needs to backtrack.

The exact training methods vary, depending on the search group and the needs of the individual dogs, but they also depend on the type of scenting technique the dog will use. Some dogs track missing people by following a scent trail on the ground. Other dogs follow air scents to locate

A canine member of a search-and-rescue team hunts for a ground scent in the Arizona desert. Humans shed about 40,000 skin cells per minute, which leaves a scent trail for dogs to follow.

people. In both cases, the training program progresses through a number of steps, each one increasing in difficulty until the dog learns how to locate missing persons.

Dogs that follow ground scents work in a tracking harness with a long line attached to it. This allows the handler to keep control of the dog while still giving the dog plenty of room to work the track. When training a tracking dog, the person laying the track (called a "track-layer") may leave some treats in his or her footprints. At first, there may be treats in every other footprint, but later on, the tracklayer will space the treats five or more footprints apart. Naturally, the dog receives treats and plenty of praise when he finds the tracklayer at the end of the track. The tracklayer may also leave scent-

ed clothing and other articles along the track for the dog to find. As the dog progresses in his training, the tracks become more complicated, with turns and cross-tracks from other people, designed to throw the dog off the scent. The dog will also progress to tracking on different types of surfaces, like concrete, gravel, and difficult terrain.

By contrast, dogs that do air scent tracking tend to work off-leash. This is a good job for herding dogs, because they work well at a distance from their handlers. Training begins with a tracklayer who excites the dog with a toy and then runs off, upwind, to hide. The dog is then released to find the tracklayer. Praise, playtime, and/or treats await the dog that makes a successful find. Because air scent dogs work off-leash and can cover ground quite a bit faster than their handlers, they have to learn to return to their handlers and lead them back to the find.

Volunteer search and rescue groups may have slightly different training programs and operating procedures. Some groups form teams that consist of a dog, a handler, and two flankers. The flankers assist in the search by carrying supplies, watching for hazards, and watching for signals from the dog. Although some groups implement their own

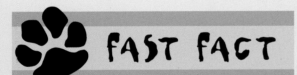

FAST FACT

While it is possible to train a ground tracking dog to do air scent searches, it is not as easy to teach an air scenting dog to do ground tracking. Air scenting comes more naturally to most dogs, and once a dog learns to use his scenting capacities this way, it is difficult to teach him to perform the more time-consuming and meticulous ground scent tracking.

certification programs, most programs follow the standards established by the National Association for Search and Rescue (NASAR).

DISASTER SURVIVORS: Similar to searching for missing persons, the search for disaster survivors involves locating a human scent; however, the disaster search dog isn't required to follow a trail. Instead, the dog simply has to have an extremely tenacious drive to locate human scent. Dogs that work disaster sites must have a lot of energy and a strong play drive to keep them motivated to search for up to 12 hours a day.

Prior obedience training is a prerequisite for any type of search work, but disaster search dogs also benefit from agility training. Learning how to navigate agility obstacles like ramps, ladders, jumps, and tunnels helps the dog develop fitness and balance that is necessary for working on unstable ground. A disaster dog needs to be able to navigate potentially dangerous terrain created by collapsed buildings, mudslides, floods, and earthquakes. Search training techniques include playing hide-and-seek games with the dog.

A rescue dog and his handler search for a missing person on the flooded Red River.

Since disaster dogs conduct their searches off-leash, they also have to learn directional commands, so their handlers can tell them where to go and where to search. Hunting and herding breeds tend to do well in this kind of search work.

Ongoing training for a search and rescue dog can be demanding, with two to six hours per week in group training sessions and additional time spent training at home. Although local volunteer search organizations are responsible for organizing group training sessions, the Federal Emergency Management Agency (FEMA) has set the standards by which disaster dogs are certified. FEMA requires dogs and handlers to become recertified every two years.

CADAVERS: Cadaver dogs, also called human remains detection (HRD) dogs, probably perform the least glamorous work of all the search dogs. Locating deceased persons is not a pleasant job, but it is necessary, nonetheless. Finding human remains helps to answer questions, solve crimes, and bring closure to loved ones.

In many situations that call for the skills of a cadaver dog, searchers do not know if the victim is alive or dead, such as in wilderness searches for missing persons. Because of this, cadaver dogs are trained to locate both living and dead subjects. After receiving training in locating missing persons, cadaver dogs learn to recognize and seek out the scent of cadav-

A cadaver dog searches for human remains in a New Orleans home destroyed by Hurricane Katrina in September 2005.

er materials, which may include human bones, hair, teeth, soft tissues, and blood. Since cadaver materials are a biohazard, trainers must adhere to very strict handling and storage procedures—they must use latex gloves when handling the materials and take steps to avoid contaminating the materials. They must also obtain the permission of law enforcement officials to use human cadaver materials for training purposes.

Training consists of introducing the dog to cadaver materials by allowing the dog to investigate the materials on his own and rewarding him when he shows interest in them. As training progresses, the dog must try to locate hidden cadaver materials. Trainers strive to simulate real-life situations, by burying cadaver materials in the soil for the dog to find, for instance. Some dogs learn to locate these materials in water as well. Depending on the dog's natural reaction to the scent materials, he may learn to respond with an aggressive or a passive alert. Certification for cadaver dogs is available through the National Association for Search and Rescue (NASAR) and the National Narcotic Detector Dog Association (NNDDA).

ESCAPED PRISONERS: Tracking down escaped prisoners is a highly specialized type of canine scent work. Dogs trained for this work must have remarkable persistence, because they may have to follow a scent trail for many miles. Bloodhounds have proven to be far superior to any other breed of dog in this line of work.

Man-tracking dogs learn to track escaped prisoners much the same way that dogs learn how to find missing persons. So it's not unusual for this type of scenting dog to work both missing persons and escaped prisoner cases. Since a man-tracking dog must pursue a particular person's scent, an article of clothing that was worn by the escaped prisoner is presented to the dog so he can smell it. The dog then attempts to locate and follow that scent from the last place the person was known to be. This type of tracking dog needs to be exceptionally fit and able to track through all types of terrain and weather.

PROTECTION

The most impressive of canine security functions is protection. Images of a snarling, snapping, fang-bearing dog can strike fear in the bravest human, and that is part of the dog's effectiveness as a protector—a protection dog's reputation alone may serve as an effective crime deterrent. But canine protection work isn't about aggression: It actually requires a high level of training, discipline, and skill.

OBEDIENCE: The foundation of protection training is obedience training. A protection dog without a solid background in obedience is like a firearm without a safety lock. Protection dog trainers recognize that the dog, as a tool, is safe and useful only when he is controllable. Obedience training installs the "on" and "off" switches for the dog's behaviors. It gives the dog's handler on-leash and off-leash control so that, in the throes of an adrenaline-packed situation, the handler still wields power over the dog's actions.

The five basic obedience commands are "Sit," "Stay," "Down," "Come," and "Heel." While the dog must be able to respond to these commands with precision before commencing protection training, the ability to control a dog goes beyond these basic skills. Protection dog handlers must also address any problem behaviors, such as jumping up, excessive barking, and any other behavior that undermines the handler's control. Some protection dog training programs even require each canine candidate to acquire an AKC Canine Good Citizen certificate. This certificate calls for valuable social and handling skills.

PERSONAL PROTECTION: Personal protection is what a dog provides when he defends his owner or property against an assailant or intruder. This is different from police dog training, because it does not necessarily require a dog to search for and "hold" a person for his handler to apprehend. In protection training, there are many different skills a dog can learn, including how to bite a person's arm if that person is holding a weapon, how to provide a defensive zone around his handler to keep an assailant away, and how to handle two or more assailants simultaneously. The exact skills depend on the individual training program and the level of the dog's skill.

FAST FACT

Many police dog trainers and personal protection dog trainers import dogs from Germany, Belgium, and other European countries for their programs. This is because most breeders in the United States cultivate dogs for show or pet qualities, rather than working qualities. As a result, domestically bred dogs tend to lack the intensely serious work ethic of many working breeds produced in Europe.

Bite work involves teaching a dog to bite an armed attacker. To properly teach this skill, a trainer must hone the dog's prey drive, so that the dog is able to react with controlled aggression when confronted by danger.

Protection dogs may learn specific fighting skills, like how to transfer their bite to a different part of the body to give them an advantage. They may learn to respond to their handlers' directions as to what part of the body to target. They may also learn to bite only at the direction of their handler, thereby removing any discretion from the dog. Regardless of their differences, all protection dog training programs must emphasize obedience to the "Out" command, which tells the dog when to release his bite.

It may take several months to two years to train a protection dog, depending on the number and complexity of the skills the dog must learn. For many protection dog owners, protection training isn't something that ends at a certain point; it is an ongoing activity that reaches progressively higher levels. Regular practice helps to keep the protection dog's skills sharp. Since protection training programs are so diverse and there is no standardized certification program for personal protection dogs, dog owners must evaluate and scrutinize training programs carefully before choosing one that will meet their needs.

POLICE WORK: Police dogs learn some of the same biting skills as personal protection dogs, but their line of work requires additional skills that help them search for, apprehend, and hold suspects until their handlers arrive. In other words, their job is not simply to protect their handler; they must actively pursue the "bad guys." Police dog training also includes agility work on various obstacles, so that the dog will be physically capable of pursuing suspects in all types of situations.

Police dogs learn where to bite a person and how to use their momentum and weight to their advantage. They also receive extra training in how to work in public places and amid lots of distractions, since they need to be exceptionally reliable in public. Because of the importance of their jobs and the high level of skill required, including skills in search and detection work, police dogs usually participate in ongoing weekly training sessions that may last two hours or longer.

Certifications for police dogs are offered through several organizations, including the U.S. Police Canine Association (USPCA), the International Police Work Dog Association (IPWDA), and the National Narcotic Detector Dog Association (NNDDA). Certification does more than test a police dog's proficiency in his job skills; it also provides liability protection for law enforcement agencies, and gives a measure of credibility to the dog when a case goes to court.

PROTECTION TRAINING AS A SPORT

The first tests of a working police dog's protection skills were developed in Germany in 1903. Breeders used these tests to evaluate and choose dogs for their breeding programs. Although the tests originally focused on the capabilities of police dogs, they attracted a lot of interest from private dog owners as well; thus the sport of Schutzhund was born. From Schutzhund evolved similar protection dog sports like the AKC working dog sport, the popular European competition known as ring sport, and the all-encompassing sport of mondioring.

SCHUTZHUND: Schutzhund, which means "protection dog" in German, has now become a world standard in evaluating a dog's working capabilities. There are three components to the Schutzhund test—obedience, tracking, and protection—and there are three levels of competition that offer progressively more difficult challenges.

Even at the Schutzhund I level, advanced off-leash skills, like heeling and retrieving over a hurdle, are required, in addition to tracking and protection tests. It takes a lot of training and practice just to achieve this first-level title. Dogs that pass this test may go on to earn a Schutzhund II title.

At the Schutzhund II level, the obedience, tracking, and protection tests are similar to those for Schutzhund I, but they require a higher level of skill and discipline. Scenting tracks are older and more complicated, obstacles in the obedience test are more difficult, and a greater amount of precision and control are required in protection work.

The Schutzhund III title is reserved for superior dogs that have already passed the Schutzhund I and Schutzhund II tests. The dog must be able to follow a track that is at least 60 minutes old and involves several turns and cross-tracks. The protection part of this test, which encompasses search and tracking, includes finding a hiding person, pursuing an escaping person, and protecting the handler when he is attacked.

Since this type of dog sport requires the dog to have a very stable temperament, a judge must evaluate a dog's temperament and obedience skills before the dog can participate. The German organization DVG (Deutscher Verband der Gebauchshundsportvereine) governs this sport worldwide. More information is available on the website for the American branch of this organization, www.dvgamerica.com.

AKC WORKING DOG SPORT: The American Kennel Club (AKC) has its own version of Schutzhund competition, called working dog sport. The test components and requirements are similar to Schutzhund, but the scoring and titling are different. In working dog sport, dogs earn the following designations after their names: WD 1, WD 2, and WD 3.

Although such sports do not necessarily provide adequate training for a dog to do police work or personal protection, they do help dog owners develop their dogs' natural abilities. They keep dogs physically fit and mentally stimulated, and they contin-

Canine sports like Schutzhund provide great training for police and security dogs.

ue to provide a method to evaluate dogs for working ability so that breeders can preserve working traits in the dogs they produce. The AKC has a complete regulation guide on working dog sport available on its website, www.akc.org.

RING SPORT: There are a number of different ring sports throughout the world, but the most popular in America is French ring sport. This dog sport incorporates many of the same elements as Schutzhund, except for tracking. Instead of having a tracking component, it has a stronger agility component, which incorporates a high jump and a long jump. The protection phase of this test includes attacking an assailant who's holding a gun and guarding an object the handler designates.

This sport is a good choice for dog owners who do not have an interest in or a use for tracking skills. Its popularity is growing rapidly among working dog owners, and new French ring sport clubs continue to proliferate in America. The national organization to contact for more information is the American Ringsport Federation at www.frenchringsport.com.

MONDIORING: The newest working dog sport is mondioring, which start-ed in the late 1980s and had its first trial in the United States in 2000. This sport combines elements of many different working dog sports throughout the world, including Schutzhund, French ring sport, KNPV (Royal Dutch Police Dog Association), and Belgian ring sport. The original organizers of the sport wanted to incorporate the best of all these different disciplines and offer an international platform for competitive working dogs.

Although still in its infancy, mondioring continues to inspire the formation of new clubs in the United States. The U.S. Mondioring Association governs the sport in this country and provides resources on its website, www.usmondioring.org.

❧❧❧❧

Dogs can be trained to assist people in many different ways, but there is no canine profession as noble as that of security. Preserving human life appears to be a destiny carved out for the dog well before he became a specialist in detection, tracking, and protection: The dog possesses both the natural talents for the job and the ability to learn how to use those talents. All of humankind is fortunate to have found such a bright and gifted friend.

CHAPTER FOUR

Jobs for Security Dogs

Canine security specialties evolved from changes in human society. Our ever-growing needs, our exploration of the depths of canine capabilities, and innovative ideas on how to utilize our canine friends to our best advantage have all opened new doors for dogs. We can now use dogs to sniff out bedbugs and ter-

mites. We can use dogs to comfort and improve the emotional and physical health of both children and adults. And when it comes to the dog's traditional job of protection, we are constantly developing new ways to hone this innate talent.

Today, there are numerous government agencies, businesses, and

The sensitive nose of this police dog can find hidden drugs during vehicle inspections.

Today there are about 4,000 military working dogs in the U.S. armed forces.

individuals that offer employment for security dogs. The breeds of dog that excel in these various positions will never be at risk of extinction as long as dangers continue to lurk in the world. From military or law enforcement service to airport security, homeland security, arson investigation, and search and rescue, security

dogs make the world a little bit safer and give us the freedom to live without fear.

MILITARY

Dogs are natural soldiers. They have built-in (and very effective) weapons. They have speed and strength and agility. They're intelligent and adaptable. Most important, they're good at following orders. Could we ask for any better companion to help us defend our country?

HISTORY OF DOGS IN WAR: It probably wasn't a big leap for the dog to transition from personal protection to military work, but it did take an imposing dog to get the ball rolling. The large Molossers, developed by the Assyrians and Persians and later adopted by the Romans, proved to have the wherewithal to become war dogs. Their size was a distinct advantage when faced with adversaries mounted on horses. These ancient war dogs were often fitted with chain mail armor and spiked collars, and their job was to attack the enemy's cavalry.

The Romans used war dogs extensively. Due to their widespread conquests, the Romans were also responsible for dispersing their war dogs throughout many nations surrounding the Mediterranean Sea.

During the Middle Ages, large fighting dogs became valued gifts for European royalty, which helped war dogs find their way into every country in Europe.

After the advent of gunpowder, war dogs were no longer as effective as they once had been. Although the use of large, powerful fighting dogs in battle diminished, many large dog breeds became private estate protection dogs. Dogs did not find new military opportunities until World War I, when they began to serve as messengers and draft animals. Germany, in particular, began to experiment with the dog's military capabilities and started using dogs extensively as sentries and guard dogs.

This kind of military work required a smaller type of war dog, one that was more agile and versatile. German Shepherds, Doberman Pinschers, and Rottweilers—all German breeds—were well-qualified for the job. After witnessing the

U.S. Marines patrol the jungle on a Pacific island with their dogs during World War II, circa 1943.

effectiveness of the German war dogs in World War I, the United States employed its own war dogs during World War II. The U.S. Marine Corps adopted the Doberman Pinscher as its dog of choice; these dogs served primarily as sentries, messengers, and guard dogs. In the mid–twentieth century, as dogs became better accepted in the U.S. military, German Shepherds began to be trained and deployed as war dogs.

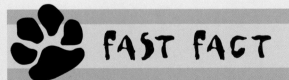

FAST FACT

A Belgian Malinois named Cairo was instrumental in taking down the infamous terrorist Osama Bin Laden in May 2011.

HOW MILITARY DOGS PROTECT US TODAY: Dogs have continued to fill many roles in the military ever since. They serve as scouts to detect hidden enemies or enemy camps. They detect bombs and guard prisoners. Since the military employs its own police force, some military dogs receive the same kind of training as police dogs, including training in tracking suspects and detecting drugs. Their service in the military is invaluable: There is no mechanical device that can detect explosives better than a dog's nose.

THE PERFECT DOG FOR THE JOB: Today, many different breeds find employment in the military. Historically, the most popular mili-

RE-HOMING RETIRED MILITARY DOGS

Private owners donated many of the dogs the military used in World War I. After the war, the majority of these dogs were retrained and sent back to their original homes or adopted by new owners. The majority of dogs that served in the Vietnam War, however, were considered expendable equipment, and they were euthanized after the war.

In 2000, President Bill Clinton signed a law that now allows private owners to adopt military dogs when their term of duty is over. Unfortunately, this law does not provide for the expense to transport the dogs home from foreign countries. An adopter must be willing to pay these expenses, which can run $2,000 or more.

There is currently a grassroots effort to pass an amendment that would require the military to classify war dogs as "canine veterans" rather than "military equipment," so that the military will have to provide transport home for these dogs. If you want to get involved in this worthy cause, visit the Military Working Dogs Adoption website, www.militaryworkingdogadoptions.com, or the Military Working Dog Foundation website, www.militaryworkingdogs.com.

tary dog breed was the German Shepherd, but there is currently a trend toward slightly smaller breeds, like the Belgian Malinois and the Dutch Shepherd. The U.S. military commonly uses Labrador Retrievers, Golden Retrievers, and Chesapeake Bay Retrievers for bomb detection and search and rescue.

LAW ENFORCEMENT

Dogs have been "crime stoppers" since they first started to protect humans, but when they began to fill this role in a more professional way, they were no longer personal protectors; they became public servants. It's impossible to speculate as to how many crimes might have gone unsolved, how many suspects might have gotten away, or how many more people might have been killed or injured if it were not for the valiant service of police dogs. What started out as a simple job for an aggressive dog has become a challenging occupation reserved only for the most capable canine.

Because of their extremely sensitive noses, police dogs can be trained to sniff out drugs and other contraband.

HISTORY OF DOGS IN LAW ENFORCEMENT: Belgian police first employed police dogs back in 1859. Germany began to test the potential of canines as law enforcers before the end of the 1800s. Both of these countries still produce some of the best police dogs in the world.

Initially, police dogs provided safe escort for night watchmen, and it didn't take much more than an aggressive canine temperament to perform this job. Of course, it always helped if the dog had a massive size and a fearsome countenance as well, since intimidation was part of the job description. But while these dogs kept night watchmen safe, they weren't always trustworthy in public. It was only a matter of time before law enforcement personnel would attempt to distill the qualities that made these canine bodyguards good partners in keeping streets safe.

While Belgian breeders developed four different varieties of Belgian Shepherd, German breeders refined the German Shepherd, Rottweiler, and Doberman Pinscher. Germany, however, made the greatest strides in training programs for police dogs. The first German Shepherd Dog club, the Verein für Deutsche Schaferhunde (SV), organized the first Schutzhund trial in 1901 as a way for German breeders to evaluate their breeding stock for working dog qualities. Other countries subsequently adopted the Schutzhund test to evaluate their own working dogs for suitability in police or military work.

HOW POLICE DOGS PROTECT US TODAY: Today, police dogs are employed all over the world, and most are granted the same rights and privileges that are afforded to human police officers. They are sworn officers, wear badges, and receive awards and commendations for their heroism. Police dogs killed in the line of duty may receive a burial with full police honors.

Police dogs can serve their communities in many different ways, including drug detection, providing protection for police officers, searching for and apprehending suspects, and searching for missing persons. They also help police departments in

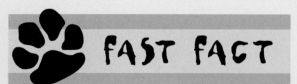

FAST FACT

A study conducted by the Department of Animal Science and Ethology at the Czech University of Life Sciences found that police dogs can distinguish between the scents of identical twins, even though identical twins share the same DNA.

indirect ways. They help foster good relations between police officers and the community, as they generate a lot of interest and open the lines of communication between law enforcement and the public. Who can resist meeting a real live police dog? Police dogs often participate in public demonstrations and educational programs for children, which helps to foster a positive image for police departments.

THE PERFECT DOG FOR THE JOB: The German Shepherd has long been the favorite breed for police work. While many other breeds possess some of the ideal traits for police work, the German Shepherd embodies all these traits in a single dog. Members of this breed have the size,

athleticism, drive, intelligence, and trainability that make them the perfect candidates for police work.

In recent years, Belgian Malinois and Dutch Shepherds have also become quite popular as police recruits. Their temperaments and drive are similar to those of German Shepherds, but they have a slightly smaller size, which makes them a little more agile and easier to handle.

AIRPORT SECURITY

Any type of port is an open door for trouble, including airports. Besides serving as entrance points for smuggled drugs and other types of contraband, they are gateways to enter the country for criminals and those bent on terrorism, and the conveyances they use—including airliners and

During the past decade, the Belgian Malinois has emerged as one of the most popular dog breeds trained for police work. These sturdy, hard-working dogs are friendly, protective, active, and relatively easy to train.

ships—are targets for bombs, hijackings, and other terrorist activities. Only through vigilant inspections can we prevent such people from victimizing innocent citizens, and the dog is there to help us foil their plots.

HISTORY OF DOGS IN AIRPORT SECURITY: The first airplane hijacking occurred in 1930, when Peruvian revolutionaries took over a Pan American flight. But it wasn't until the early 1970s that airport security became a serious concern. A number of hijackings and bombings spurred the Federal Aviation Administration (FAA) to draft new security rules that called for the scanning of baggage and passengers. Included in

these beefed-up security arrangements was the implementation of the Explosives Detection Canine Team program in 1973. This program began with 40 canine teams, distributed among 20 airports. These changes in airport security significantly reduced the incidence of air piracy (hijacking) and bombings.

The FAA implemented improvements in airport security in the 1990s, which included the addition of x-ray machines, extra personnel, and new scanning equipment. By 1997 the number of Explosives Detection Canine Teams had grown to 87. Unfortunately, such measures were not enough to prevent the terrorist hijackings and crashes of four

Since 2008, the Transportation Security Administration (TSA) has trained more than 400 dog-handler teams to search for bomb materials in cargo as part of its National Explosives Detection Canine Team Program. TSA is the government agency responsible for protecting the nation's transportation systems so Americans can travel safely.

U.S. airliners on September 11, 2001, two of which destroyed the Twin Towers in New York City and one of which crashed into the Pentagon in Virginia.

Shortly after the 9/11 attacks, the Transportation Security Administration (TSA) was formed to oversee our nation's airport security. This government entity is now responsible for the administration of the Explosives Detection Canine Program, and the number of explosives detection dogs working in airports has increased exponentially.

How Airport Security Dogs Protect Us Today:
Bomb-sniffing dogs in airports have taken on more responsibilities than ever before. They no longer only check baggage; they also inspect cargo holds, vehicles, and airport terminals. They are available to respond to bomb threats, and their presence at airport facilities serves as a deterrent for criminals and terrorists.

The TSA currently provides training in explosives detection for dogs and handlers. It offers training aids, reimbursement for expenses related to the program, funding for research to improve the efficiencies of the program, and certification for dogs and handlers. According to the TSA, bomb-sniffing dogs still remain the

FAST FACT

There is currently a debate as to which is more effective and economical in detecting bomb materials at airports—bomb-sniffing dogs or full body scanners. Dogs may very well prove to be more practical than high-tech equipment for this job.

most accurate and reliable method of explosives detection in airport security.

The Perfect Dog for the Job:
The TSA operates a breeding program to produce dogs for its Explosives Detection Canine Team program. The TSA Canine Breeding and Development Center, located at Lackland Air Force Base in San Antonio, Texas, is modeled after a very successful Australian program, called the Australian Customs Service National Breeding and Development Centre. Foster families raise the puppies until they are old enough to undergo specialized training when they are a year old. Some of the breeds produced in this program include Labrador Retrievers, German Shepherds, Belgian Malinois, and Viszlas, because of their superior scenting abilities and their predisposition for this type of work.

U.S. CUSTOMS AND BORDER SECURITY (HOMELAND SECURITY)

The United States has a well-deserved reputation as a welcoming nation, accepting immigrants and visitors from many foreign countries, as well as conducting trade in a worldwide market. However, with such an open-door policy, it is very difficult to prevent illegal drugs, counterfeit or pirated products, illegal aliens, or terrorists from entering the country. The U.S. Customs and Border Protection (CBP) agency stands guard at entry points and monitors everything that comes across our borders. CBP is responsible for providing safeguards that allow for free travel and trade without putting U.S. citizens at risk. Dogs have supported this mission for almost half a century.

HISTORY OF U.S. CUSTOMS AND BORDER SECURITY: In order to address the problem of drug smuggling, the U.S. Customs Service (the predecessor of CPB) began a program to train dogs in the detection of narcotics in 1970. The U.S. Border Patrol (another earlier agency, since merged into CPB) launched its own canine detection program in 1986 to detect both humans (illegal immigrants) and illegal drugs. Each of these agencies built, maintained, and operated their own training facilities.

In 2003, the U.S. Customs Service and the U.S. Border Patrol were united as part of the newly formed Department of Homeland Security (DHS). The U.S. Immigration and Naturalization Service and the Animal Plant Health Inspection Service (a division of the U.S. Department of Agriculture) also fell under DHS in the government reorganization. The two canine training facilities of the U.S. Customs Service and the U.S. Border Patrol then became consolidated under the

U.S. Customs and Border Protection (CBP) Office of Training and Development.

Dogs in the CBP program are trained in one of several areas of specialization, which include concealed humans and narcotics detection, passenger processing narcotics detection, search and rescue, and currency and firearms detection. Concealed humans and narcotics detection involves inspecting premises as well as any conveyances that carry freight, luggage, or mail. Passenger processing narcotics detection focuses on inspecting arriving passengers or pedestrians and the items they carry with them. Search and rescue canines receive training in locating people lost in wilderness areas. And currency and firearms detection specifically focuses on searching for large quantities of currency or firearms that represent criminal activity.

The U.S. Department of Agriculture operates a third canine training program separately, for its own purposes, in Atlanta. Dogs in this program learn to detect prohibited meat, fruit, plant material, and ani-

This U.S. Customs and Border Patrol canine is screening suitcases on an airport luggage belt.

mal products that could cause health risks to humans or damage to domestic agriculture. These dogs inspect cargo that is transported in a variety of conveyances, including automobiles, trucks, buses, and airplanes.

How Customs and Border Patrol Security Dogs Protect Us Today: The CBP currently employs 1,500 canine teams throughout the country, which makes it the largest law enforcement canine program in the nation. Dogs receive training in a variety of specialties that help them protect our country from a wide range of threats that can cross our borders. Trained dog teams work in many ports of entry, including seaports, airports, and land ports of entry.

The Best Dog for the Job: The CBP employs a variety of breeds in national security work, including Labrador Retrievers, Golden Retrievers, German Shepherds, Belgian Malinois, and many mixed breeds. The CBP currently obtains up to 20 percent of its dogs from animal shelters, private breeders, and private owners who donate their pets. The CBP also recruits dogs from its own breeding program.

The U.S. Department of Agriculture favors Beagles for airport work because of their small size, gentle disposition, and excellent scenting ability. The "Beagle Brigade" inspects airport baggage for contraband foodstuffs. For inspecting larger areas, like airport cargo areas or mail distribution centers, the Department of Agriculture uses larger-breed dogs.

ARSON INVESTIGATION

Humans can certainly live without dogs, but our lives are much easier when dogs are available to assist us. Arson investigation is one field where dogs save us both time and expense. Without use of the dog's remarkable nose to pinpoint areas where accelerants have been used to start fires, arson investigators would have to collect a lot more samples from fire scenes to be tested for accelerants. Besides demanding more of the inspector's time, the expense to test all these samples would be considerably higher.

History of Canine Arson Investigation: The Bureau of Alcohol, Tobacco and Firearms (ATF) first looked into the use of canines to detect accelerants in arson cases in 1984. A collaboration between the ATF and the Connecticut State Police produced the first official arson dog, a Labrador Retriever named Mattie. The program was such a success that the ATF established the National Canine Accelerant Detection Program in 1989. This program now provides approximately 50 accelerant detection canine teams throughout the country.

Another accelerant detection canine training program, the Arson Dog Program, began in 1993 with funding from State Farm Insurance. Maine Specialty Dogs, a training facility, trains the dogs in this program according to the guidelines set by the Maine Criminal Justice Academy. This program has placed over 200 canine teams in 41 states, the District of Columbia, and Canada.

HOW ARSON DETECTION DOGS PROTECT US TODAY: Today, there are a number of ways arson investigators can acquire the services of an accelerant detection dog. Some municipalities implement their own training programs and construct their own canine teams. Private training facilities may train accelerant detection dogs and then provide trained dogs or arson detection services to arson investigators. A fire department delegate may take part in the Arson Dog Program by enrolling through the Maine Criminal Justice Academy. The ATF continues to maintain its training program for accelerant detection

dogs, which it provides to state and local fire departments, police departments, and fire marshals' offices in cases that call for ATF involvement.

The duties of arson detection dogs have gone beyond inspecting fire scenes. They may also be called on to inspect vehicles, clothing, containers, and even people to determine if accelerants are present. The dogs are often available 24 hours a day so they may provide service at a moment's notice.

THE BEST DOG FOR THE JOB: As is the case with most canine security jobs, the best dog for arson detection work depends on specific traits, rather than a specific breed; however, Labrador Retrievers comprise the majority of dogs in this field. Their scenting abilities, friendly temperaments, trainability, and play drive make them exceptionally well-suited

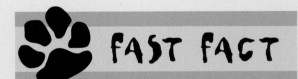

FAST FACT

Arson dogs may be trained to give different kinds of alerts. A primary alert may consist of sitting near the site of the scent. A secondary alert will be more specific as to the location of the scent, with the dog actively sniffing where the scent is located.

to this job. Arson detection dog training often includes food rewards, and Labradors tend to be highly motivated by food. The Golden Retriever comes in a close second as an ideal choice for arson detection duty. Both of these breeds have been highly successful in helping to solve crimes of arson.

SEARCH AND RESCUE

Unlike most other canine security jobs, search and rescue (SAR) work is rarely a paid job for dog handlers, even though search and rescue is arguably the most difficult kind of

A handler gives a hug to a FEMA search and rescue dog in Atlanta.

canine security work. Working conditions may be brutal, with harsh weather, dangerous and unstable footing, and treacherous terrain. Searches may be both physically and emotionally draining. Yet, volunteers are willing to invest enormous amounts of precious time to train their dogs, in addition to covering their own expenses for travel and equipment, in order to provide life-saving search and rescue services.

HISTORY OF CANINE SEARCH AND RESCUE: Dogs have probably searched for and rescued humans since the beginning of their relationship with us, but the monks of St. Bernard's Pass were the first to provide formal training for search and rescue dogs. St. Bernard's Pass was a treacherous route through the Alps; many travelers traversing the pass got lost or were buried in avalanches. By the early 1700s, the large dogs owned and trained by the monks were the best hope for those who encountered problems on their journey. The dogs, now called St. Bernards, were superior in locating humans, digging up people buried in the snow, and providing warmth for those who lost their way.

Beginning with World War I, military forces began to use dogs to locate and rescue wounded soldiers.

This was a stepping-stone to using dogs for search and rescue domestically. Local search and rescue clubs began to form for the purpose of providing services for the public. In 1972, Bill and Jean Syrotuck, dog trainers from Washington State, formed the first national search and rescue organization, the American Rescue Dog Association (ARDA). This organization helped to unite search and rescue groups across the nation so they could benefit from their collective resources.

How Search and Rescue Dogs Protect Us Today: There are now a number of national organizations besides ARDA that provide support and resources for canine search and rescue teams, including the Search Dog Foundation (SDF), the National Association for Search and Rescue (NASAR), and Search and Rescue Dogs of the United States (SARDUS). There are many local organizations as well.

Search and rescue dogs assist in many different types of searches, including wilderness, disaster, cadaver, avalanche, and water searches. Each of these specialties requires a different set of skills. Search and rescue dog teams may respond to the needs of local law enforcement or, in the case of a disaster, to the Federal Emergency Management Agency (FEMA).

The Perfect Dog for the Job: The most common breeds of dog that FEMA certifies for disaster work are the German Shepherd, the Labrador Retriever, the Golden Retriever, the Belgian Malinois, and the Border Collie. These same breeds tend to dominate many canine security fields; however, there is always a small minority of exceptions. Since most search and rescue handlers are civilians, a large variety of breeds enter search and rescue training programs, including mixed breeds. Even though few will eventually qualify for advanced certification, there are always a few shining stars that come from nontraditional breeds.

Modern security dogs protect us in so many ways that it's hard to imagine a safe world without them. Who would have thought, a thousand years ago, that the dog's protective nature would have evolved into a profession with as many facets as a brilliant-cut diamond? No doubt, we will continue to find new uses for the dog's extraordinary talents, providing even more proof of the dog's value to humankind.

CHAPTER five

Personal Protection Dogs

One of the greatest rewards of dog ownership is the steadfast companionship dogs have to offer. They have earned the title of "our best friend" for good reason, but imagine if your dog could be much more than just a fantastic buddy. What if he could also earn his keep? Personal protection dogs provide security as well as unconditional love.

Dog ownership is not a simple consideration, regardless of the breed of dog that captures your interest. You must be willing to make concessions in your lifestyle in order to accommodate a canine family member, and these concessions may be significant. In the case of personal protection dogs, however, there are even more concerns. Will you be able to control a strong-bodied and strong-willed

This dog is obeying a command given by his handler to take a defensive position.

dog? Will you have the time to train a personal protection dog? Is your living situation one that will meet the needs of a personal protection dog without causing conflicts for humans? Your reasons for owning a protection dog may be valid, but you'll need to determine if this type of dog is a good fit for your entire life, not just a part of it.

LIFESTYLE CONSIDERATIONS: The biggest consideration in getting any dog is the time required to care for, train, exercise, clean up after, and provide companionship for your canine pal. Protective dog breeds tend to require a greater time commitment than other dogs. They are medium to large size, which means there is more work involved in grooming and cleaning up after them. The working dog breeds also tend to have higher energy levels, and they need plenty of exercise to let off steam. Most of them are famously loyal to their special people, and they are happiest when they can spend a lot of companionship time with their owners.

Protective dog breeds also require a great deal of time for training. Some dogs are naturally respectful and submissive, and can become perfect pets with little training at all, but this is not the case with protective

FAST FACT

Due to their typically assertive, strong-minded personalities, most protective dog breeds are not recommended for first-time dog owners. Previous experience in dog training and handling allows prospective dog owners to determine if a protective breed of dog is right for them.

dog breeds. Independent-minded dogs always require obedience training in order for them to gain control over their behavior, but personal protection dogs, in particular, need to have a solid education in obedience before they will be ready for protection training. Once a dog is specially trained in protection skills, he will also require continuing education.

In other words, protective dog breeds are not a good choice for people who have extremely busy lives or demanding jobs. In addition to the time it takes to train them, these dogs may require an hour or more of play and exercise time per day, and this requirement will have to take priority over the dog owner's other activities and interests. While police dogs and military dogs can look forward to doing a strenuous job every day, the typical canine house pet lives a relatively sedentary and boring lifestyle that is not very satisfying for a working dog. These dogs need to follow a daily exercise regimen. Are you prepared to offer that?

The dog's size may also pose challenges, as bigger dogs take up more room. They can easily knock down small children, especially when the dogs are still young and boisterous. And it may be difficult to physically control a large, powerful dog, especially for elderly people. Take everyone in your household into consideration when choosing a suitable dog for your living situation, and make sure everyone is agreeable to getting a large dog.

You may also need to consider the other pets in your household. The prey drive in protective breeds can be quite high, and some of these dogs may not get along well with smaller animals, like house cats. If you have other pets, it is best to introduce a dog to your household on a trial basis to be sure he will get along with your other furry companions.

LIABILITY CONSIDERATIONS:

Protective dog breeds aren't any more likely to bite people than other breeds of dog. In fact, the journal *Applied Animal Behavior Science* published a study in 2008 indicating that Dachshunds, Chihuahuas, and Jack Russell Terriers (in that order)

are the breeds most likely to react aggressively toward strangers. However, the liability concerns of owning a protective breed of dog are still very real. When these large, strong dogs do bite, the damage they inflict is significantly more serious than any harm that a small dog could do. As a result, protective dog breeds have acquired fearsome reputations.

A protection dog's potential to do serious harm to a person is a liability concern, but a dog that is trained to bite creates an even greater risk. In some respects, a trained protection dog is safer than an untrained protection dog, because a trained dog has learned to control his biting behavior. Still, a dog that has bitten a human for any reason has crossed a critical line, and there is no way for him to go back. This has made it difficult to find appropriate adoptive homes for some retired police and military dogs.

Owning a bite-trained protection dog is a huge responsibility. You must be willing to train and manage your dog so that you can exercise adequate control over him. You must take precautions to prevent accidental biting. You'll also need expert guidance so you can learn how to handle your dog properly. Are you prepared to do everything it takes to minimize your liability exposure?

BREED CONSIDERATIONS: Protective dog breeds share a number of characteristics that help make them successful as guardians. Their substantial size, independent minds, strong loyalty, and natural cautiousness around strangers are qualifications for the job, but that's about as far as their similarities go. Each breed has its own unique traits that make it special, and it's important to choose a protection dog with the right traits for you.

Some protection breeds, like the Belgian Tervuren, have long, beautiful hair. Others, like the Doberman Pinscher, have short, sleek coats. Still others, like the German Shepherd, have medium-length coats. How much grooming and hair cleanup are you willing to do? In what kind of outdoor conditions will you require your dog to work?

Although all the protective breeds are large enough to get their jobs done, some have greater strength while others are gifted with more agility. Choosing a personal protection dog is not about getting the largest, most powerful dog; it's about

Children should never be left unattended around any dog.

Be aware of local laws related to ownership of personal protection dogs. Some communities require large dogs like this German Shepherd to wear a wire basket safety muzzle when out in public.

The most popular breeds in personal protection work are German Shepherds and Belgian Shepherds, which include the Belgian Malinois and the Belgian Tervuren. These breeds are easy to train and control, and they have a high aptitude for protection work. Their physical characteristics make them very versatile as both companions and protectors. However, the short, easy-care coats of Rottweilers, Dobermans, and Pit Bulls provide advantages as well. Be sure to research a breed thoroughly before making your final choice.

BREED-SPECIFIC LEGISLATION: Your choice of personal protection dog may not be entirely your own decision. Many communities now restrict the types of guard dogs their citizens may own. Breed-specific legislation (BSL) has come about because of irresponsible owners who mishandle their protective dogs and endanger the public. There are also unscrupulous breeders who care more about making a profit than about developing good dogs; these types of breeders often produce protective dogs that have unstable temperaments.

Before deciding if a particular breed is the choice for you, check with your local town or city hall to make sure there are no laws banning

choosing a dog that you can physically control. Since personal protection training requires the owner to physically restrain the dog during various exercises, a dog that is too strong for his owner to handle is a disaster waiting to happen.

the breed you desire. The most commonly banned breeds are Rottweilers and Pit Bulls, which are responsible for the greatest number of fatal canine attacks in the United States.

If your community does not currently have restrictions on guard dog ownership, do your part to discourage such discriminatory legislation by training and managing your dog properly. The breeds targeted for this type of legislation tend to suffer from a stigma that causes people to judge them before they know them. Although you can't necessarily sway the opinion of the masses, you do have the power to influence the opinions of those who live near you, those you may encounter while out for a walk with your dog, and those who visit your home. When you manage your dog in ways that respect the rights of others, you and your dog will undoubtedly leave a good impression with everyone you meet.

CHOOSING A PERSONAL PROTECTION DOG

Deciding on which breed meets your needs and personal tastes is the easy part of dog selection. Although the dogs within a certain breed share many characteristics, there is still great variation in temperament among individual dogs. Evaluating the personalities of individual dogs is

FAST FACT

When choosing a personal protection dog, keep in mind that some property and liability insurers have restrictions on the types of dogs they will cover. Insurance companies that do not have an outright ban on certain breeds have very strict policies regarding dog bite claims. Be sure to check with the carrier of your homeowner's or renter's insurance regarding policies and restrictions concerning dogs.

always important when choosing any type of dog as a pet, but it is even more critical when choosing a dog for personal protection.

Because protective breeds are so popular, and there are so many of them available through breeders, pet shops, shelters, and private owners, you'll find a huge difference in quality from one dog to another. Protective dogs with unstable temperaments or genetic health conditions do not make good pets, and they make even worse prospects for personal protection work.

EVALUATING BREEDERS: The best place to find a suitable personal protection prospect is from a reputable breeder, but would you know a good breeder if you saw one? These are some of the signs that a breeder puts a lot of effort into producing quality dogs with exemplary temperaments:

- The puppies' living environment is clean.
- The puppies have had outdoor experiences.
- The puppies appear to be clean and healthy.
- One or both parent dogs are available for inspection.
- The puppies appear to be well-socialized and are not fearful of people.
- The puppies have received their first veterinary checkup and vaccinations.
- Vaccination records, registration papers, and pedigrees are available at the time of sale.
- The results of tests for genetic health conditions, such as hip dysplasia, are available. (Be sure to research the genetic health conditions that are common for your breed of choice.)

A good breeder isn't just a good source of quality dogs; she can also be a good source of information and advice. So you'll want to be just as particular in choosing a breeder as you are in choosing your future canine protector. Your puppy's breeder may very well become your mentor in protection dog ownership.

You can locate breeders through many different sources, including veterinarians, classified ads, dog shows, and online searches, but one of the best places to find a dog with the right mettle for protection work is to check with your local protection dog trainer. You may even want to ask the trainer for assistance in choosing the right dog.

EVALUATING CANINE PERSONALITY TRAITS: You might think a personal protection dog needs to be aggressive in order to his job, but this is far from the truth. Excessive, unprovoked, or "hair-trigger" aggression is a sign of mental instability. This kind of behavior is not normal for either humans or dogs. Inappropriate canine aggression may be the result of a lack of socialization or improper handling of the dog, but it may also have its roots in genetics. Some dogs just have mean temperaments or a higher propensity to bite.

A protective dog with a stable temperament never reacts to any situation with aggression instantly or blindly. He'll take the time to think about what he's doing. He may give a warning growl first. He will not be snappy or cranky, but instead will analyze a situation or scrutinize a person's intentions before deciding how to react. Avoid any dog that seems to have a moody temperament, is impulsive, or lacks self-control.

If you are choosing a puppy, it may be difficult to determine exactly what the puppy's personality will be like as an adult. You can find the

HOW TO TREAT YOUR PROTECTIVE DOG

People are amazingly ignorant about how to treat or act around dogs. When you own a protective breed of dog, you must be willing to educate people, especially children, in the correct treatment of canines. Some of the things you may need to teach include:

- Never raise your hand above the head of a strange dog to pet him. Always let the dog sniff the back of your hand first, and when the dog is comfortable with you, you may pet him on the underside of the neck or on the chest.

- Never tease or antagonize a dog.

- Never run away from a dog that frightens you. This may excite the dog's prey drive, and prompt him to chase you. Instead, face the dog and back away slowly.

- Never enter a dog's territory (the yard or house) unannounced and uninvited. Always wait for the dog's owner to let you in.

- Never pet a strange dog without the owner's permission.

- Never attempt to pet a dog through a fence or a cage.

- Never stare directly into the eyes of a strange dog: This may represent a challenge or threat to the dog.

- Never "gang up on" a dog, corner a dog, or otherwise make a dog feel threatened.

- Always treat dogs with respect and kindness.

Jack and Wendy Volhard developed one of the best puppy personality tests available. This test can help you determine if your puppy has the right temperament for personal protection work. You can access the Puppy Aptitude Test (PAT) at www.volhard.com

best clues to a puppy's adult temperament by evaluating the puppy's sire and dam. The old adage, "The apple doesn't fall far from the tree," holds a great deal of truth.

An ideal working protection dog is bold, calm, inquisitive, and playful. A dog that is shy, timid, or fearful may react aggressively out of fear. A dog that is dominant or overly assertive may be too difficult to control. Protection work is serious business that calls for a well-balanced, forgiving temperament. Steer clear of temperament extremes that may leave you with a dog that is either "trigger happy" or reluctant to engage.

EVALUATING CANINE HEALTH: A dog with all the right physical and temperamental qualities isn't going to be of much use if he isn't healthy. When choosing a puppy or an adult dog, beware of common health con-

ditions and hereditary flaws that can sideline or terminate a dog's protection career. Inspect the dog's physical condition from head to toe, making sure there is no discharge from the eyes or nose. The dog's eyes should be bright and alert, his coat should be shiny and dandruff-free, and his ears should be clean. Any dog that appears unhealthy or lethargic is probably ill or suffering from intestinal parasites.

Many large dogs, including those from the protective breeds, experience hip dysplasia, which is a deformed hip joint. This hereditary condition may seriously impact a dog's mobility and quality of life. The Orthopedic Foundation for Animals analyzes dogs' hip x-rays and certifies dogs over the age of two that have proven to be free of this condition. You would do well to choose a dog whose parents have been certified through this organization

Become familiar with the common hereditary conditions associated

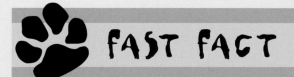

Health conditions, especially those that cause pain, can make dogs aggressive. Keep your dog healthy by taking him for regular annual veterinary exams.

Successful trainers reward obedient working dogs with playtime and affection.

with dogs of the breed you're considering adopting, so you can recognize the symptoms. Ask breeders if their dogs have any history of heritable disorders before purchasing a puppy. And always remember to have your dog checked by a veterinarian shortly after purchase.

TRAINING

The type of training personal protection dogs receive is different from that of police dogs. For instance, personal protection dogs receive defensive training only, since their jobs entail defending their owners.

There is no reason to train a personal protection dog in offensive strategies, such as pursuing, immobilizing, and holding suspects, which is part of a police dog's work. Since personal protection dogs require a special set of skills, it is imperative to choose the right training program for your dog. A competent trainer can help you turn your dog's natural instincts into a valuable tool.

EVALUATING TRAINERS: Internet searches provide the easiest and fastest way to locate protection dog trainers. Although specialized training programs for personal protection dogs may be hard to find in some areas, you should spend much more time evaluating training classes than looking for them. There are no set standards in protection dog training. Trainers do not need to possess any particular education or experience to call themselves protection dog trainers, nor are they required to use specific training techniques. Protection dog training is a completely unregulated field that requires close scrutiny by protection dog owners. Some of the things you should look for in a training class include:

- Humane training methods. There are still a few disreputable trainers who intimidate and brutalize dogs to make them mean. The dogs learn to distrust all strangers and to react violently to anyone who encroaches on their territory. Dogs trained in this way are not disciplined, trustworthy protectors.
- A temperament evaluation. A dog must have the right temperament for personal protection work. Any trainer who does not evaluate dogs before accepting them into a protection training program is a trainer you should avoid.

- A class that requires dogs to be obedience-trained. A dog is not ready for protection dog training until he is very well versed in obedience, since you must be able to control your dog when you ask him to do this type of work.
- A training class that meets your needs. Every protection dog training program is different. Some training classes go beyond teaching dogs to defend their owners and actually teach the dogs specific fighting techniques. Training classes may prepare your dog for different types of scenarios, such as an attack by more than one person. Ask trainers exactly what skills they teach in their classes, and choose one that you think will give you the kind of protection dog you want. A good trainer will tailor his program somewhat to meet your needs.
- A class that includes canine socialization. A well-socialized dog is much easier to manage and control than one that is not. Socialization helps to avoid inappropriate aggression and helps the dog to develop good judgment.

A reputable trainer will allow you to observe a class before enrolling your dog, and it is a good idea to take advantage of this. It will give you an opportunity to see firsthand what kind of training techniques the trainer uses, how the trainer interacts with the human students and dogs, and the general atmosphere of the class. It may also give you a chance to ask class participants what they like or don't like about the class. If you can't observe a class in session, ask the trainer for client references. Although a trainer is unlikely to refer you to someone who is not happy with her training program, her willingness to provide client contacts is a good indication that she runs a respectable business.

ONGOING TRAINING: Hopefully, your dog will never have to use his training. The whole purpose of training your dog in protection is to be prepared in case he ever does, but the opportunities for him to use his education in real-life situations will probably be very rare. However, if your dog never gets to practice his skills, he may eventually forget them.

Police dogs undergo regular training sessions, sometimes once a week, to keep their skills sharp. You'll need to provide ongoing training and practice for your personal protection dog,

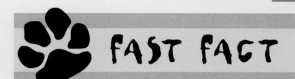

FAST FACT

Some dog trainers sell pretrained personal protection dogs. These dogs tend to be tremendously expensive, running between $20,000 and $35,000, because of the intensive training they receive. Although these dogs may be a good choice for high-profile celebrities, who can afford them and whose busy lifestyles make it impossible for them to train their own dogs, most dog owners are better off training their own dogs. Training your own dog helps to build a strong owner-dog bond, which is extremely important to protection dogs.

too. Enrolling in a refresher course once in a while can help you reinforce your control over your dog and help your dog maintain his self-discipline.

SOCIALIZATION OF THE PROTECTION DOG: The importance of socialization for a protection dog cannot be overstated. A training class that includes socialization activities is ideal, because it is important to control a protection dog while in the midst of distractions. In addition to social opportunities in training classes, get your dog out and about frequently so he can experience the world from his own four paws. Seek out distracting locations, such as dog parks, pet stores, and high-traffic areas, to train your dog so he becomes more reliable. All these experiences will ultimately help your dog develop good judgment skills as a personal protector.

SCHUTZHUND TRAINING VERSUS PROTECTION DOG TRAINING: Many people think Schutzhund training is synonymous with protection dog training. This is not the case. Schutzhund is a method of testing a dog's working ability. German dog fanciers developed this test in order to help them choose the right dogs for their breeding programs. Think of it as an aptitude test for protection dogs. Schutzhund has become a very popular sport, and it does keep dogs fit and healthy, but Schutzhund training does not necessarily prepare a dog to handle the kinds of real-life situations he may encounter as a personal protection dog.

A protection dog must be willing to bite a person on whichever arm he's using to hold a weapon, not just the arm with a padded sleeve. While Schutzhund dogs view their work as a fun game in which they never get hurt, personal protection dogs must be willing to take their job more seriously, even if it means becoming injured themselves. These differences necessitate different training scenarios. And while a Schutzhund-certified dog may be cross-trained in personal protection work, it is not always easy or practical to train a personal protection dog to engage in the sport of Schutzhund.

🐾🐾🐾

FAST FACT

Protective dogs tend to be cautious around strange people—at least until they get to know them. This is something to remember if you ever consider hiring the services of a pet sitter. Make sure your dog will accept a pet sitter into your home when you are not there. A proper introduction to the pet sitter will help facilitate a smooth interaction.

A trained personal protection dog can provide protection when needed and peace of mind the rest of the time. Although he performs a valuable service, he has a dual purpose—as both a protector and a companion. This double-duty function is one advantage that an electronic alarm system simply cannot match.

CHAPTER SIX

The Natural Protector

Y ou don't necessarily need to own a trained personal protection dog to benefit from a dog's natural protective capabilities. All dogs are protectors at heart, and even the most mild-mannered, submissive canine has the potential to become a hero under the right circumstances. If you already have a dog, and you're not sure if your dog has what it takes to protect you, think about your dog's particular characteristics.

YOUR DOG AS A PROTECTOR

Does your dog have a close bond with you? If so, he may very well defend you if you ever find yourself in a threatening situation. Does your dog like to bark? If so, he may just alert you to a house fire or burglar some day. Although you can benefit

According to recent studies, 40 percent of American dog owners acquired their pets primarily to protect their homes and families.

from your dog's natural talents, you can also suffer as a result of them. Inappropriate aggression, excessive barking, or extreme territoriality may result in everything from frazzled nerves to human injuries. Learn how to manage your dog to maximize the benefits of canine protectiveness while eliminating the drawbacks.

TERRITORIALITY: The strength of your dog's sense of territory is preset in his genes. Although all dogs possess some territorial instinct, certain dogs are more territorial than others. This instinct is useful for a couple of

Dogs must be trained not to aggressively defend territory that they consider to be their own, such as your back yard.

reasons—it makes it possible to train a dog to respect yard boundaries, and it encourages a dog to alert his owner when strangers approach or enter the yard or house. Problems may occur, however, when a dog's territorial instinct is overcharged.

Dogs with a strong territorial instinct require firm limits on how they express this instinct, or they may develop the bad habit of fence-line aggression or cause problems whenever guests attempt to enter the house. Strong canine leadership is required to make it clear to the dog that the human is in charge of deciding who is a threat, and who can or cannot enter the property. Dogs that trust their competent human leaders have little reason to make these decisions on their own.

Problems with territorial aggression may arise when a dog owner keeps a dog tethered or chained outdoors. Dogs that are kept tied to doghouses or other stationary objects are at risk of developing a dangerously high territorial response to intruders. In this case, the dog has an extremely restricted territory, and the tie itself puts the dog in a helpless, and therefore defensive, position. People (usually children) who ignorantly wander within reach of the dog then become victims of the dog's aggressive response. For safety reasons, tie-outs are not appropriate for dogs that have strong territorial instincts.

You can avoid inappropriate territorial aggression with proper canine management. Make sure your dog receives plenty of socialization so he can learn the difference between threatening and nonthreatening situations. Enforce limits on territorial behavior indoors, and provide adequate supervision outdoors. It is never a good practice to leave a dog outside unattended. Your dog may suffer from teasing, harassment, or threats from humans or other animals. Your dog needs to know that you are there to protect him so that he doesn't need to protect himself.

RESPONDING TO STRANGERS: The instinct to be cautious around strangers is rooted in survival, and it also has a connection to the dog's sense of social hierarchy. Anyone who is not included in your dog's "pack," or protected circle, is consid-

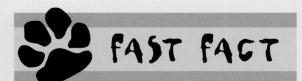

The most common breed of dog chosen as a pet for family protection is the German Shepherd.

Black or dark-colored dogs provide greater crime deterrence than those with other coat colors.

ered an outsider. Some dogs seem to think that everyone is a friend, but even these dogs may be able to differentiate between friendly strangers they meet on the street and strangers who try to break into the house in the middle of the night.

If your dog has a more protective nature, don't be surprised if he views men more suspiciously than women or children. Men tend to be larger and stronger, and they have deeper voices and behave more aggressively, all of which make them a greater threat in a dog's eyes. First impressions can mean a lot to some dogs, so make sure you introduce your dog to new people properly. Do not allow new acquaintances—whether children or adults—to tease or antagonize your dog. With sensible handling, your dog will learn to make good choices in how he uses his protective instinct.

ALERTNESS: Dogs come with all different levels of alertness. Some dogs are so sensitive that a plane flying overhead will send them into a frenzy of barking, while other dogs could easily sleep through World War III. Paradoxically, the breeds with the most protective brawn, like Mastiffs and Great Danes, tend to have the lowest level of alertness, while some of the smallest breeds, like Yorkshire Terriers and Pomeranians, are hypervigilant. Medium-sized dogs often fall between these two extremes, alerting their human companions to the majority of potential threats but missing a few.

FAST FACT

Breeds that make good watchdogs include:
- Airedale Terrier
- Cairn Terrier
- Chihuahua
- Fox Terrier
- Jack Russell Terrier
- Lhasa Apso
- Manchester Terrier
- Miniature Pinscher
- Miniature Schnauzer
- Pomeranian
- Poodle
- Schipperke
- Scottish Terrier
- Tibetan Spaniel
- West Highland White Terrier
- Yorkshire Terrier

The dichotomy between large, strong protectors and small, alert watchdogs creates a division in security dog jobs. Guard dogs assume the physical aspects of protection while watchdogs function as sentinels. A lucky dog owner might own one of each, thereby employing a watchdog to alert the guard dog and benefiting from a full-featured canine security system. For at least 800 years, the people of Tibet have utilized just such a system by keeping powerful Tibetan Mastiffs as outdoor guard dogs and small, hyperalert Lhasa Apsos as indoor sentries.

WATCHDOG OR GUARD DOG?

Perhaps you are not in a position to own more than one dog. If you had to make a choice, which would be better—a watchdog or a guard dog? Each has distinct advantages and disadvantages. You'll need to consider your living situation to determine the best choice for you.

WATCHDOGS: For the purpose of crime deterrence, a small- to medium-size watchdog is economical and practical. They are less expensive to feed, less work to clean up after, and easier to transport. Though they may be marvelously efficient at detecting and alerting their owners to potential threats, they aren't always capable of backing up their bark with an effective bite. But that isn't necessarily a bad thing.

The liability risk is much lower with a watchdog than with a guard dog, since the use of deadly force is generally not a possibility with these smaller canines. This leaves the decision about how to handle a threat up to the dog's owner, rather than the dog himself. Law enforcement agencies generally promote the ownership of watchdogs, as opposed to guard dogs, because they are safer and extremely effective in deterring criminals. After all, a dog does not need to be capable of physically addressing a threat on his own; he only needs to alert humans, who can then call 911 in an emergency.

A barking dog is one of the best security systems available. Not only can a barking dog awaken his owner; he can awaken half the neighborhood as well, and this is not something a burglar or home invader wants. Criminals try to avoid targeting homes with dogs.

To serve as an effective watchdog, a dog must be extremely alert and reactive (by barking) in the face of potentially threatening stimuli. Small, noisy dogs like Yorkshire Terriers meet these requirements.

GUARD DOGS: Still, there may be times when only a guard dog will do. A guard dog can provide a tremendous feeling of security for his owner, especially for an owner who lives in a high-crime area. A guard dog may be desirable for someone who wants a canine jogging partner that can also function as a bodyguard. Guard dogs are also a good choice for those who live alone, who live in a secluded area, or who simply prefer a larger dog. The very sight of the dog is enough to deter most robbers or burglars.

A guard dog has a naturally protective personality and doesn't need specialized training in order to do his job, although some owners do choose to educate their dogs in the finer arts of protection. Guard dogs do, however, require intensive obedience training, and this can be both expensive and time-consuming. Without proper training and discipline, guard-type dogs can become too much for even their owners to handle, and there is nothing more dangerous than an out-of-control guard dog.

MANAGING YOUR DOG'S PROTECTIVE INSTINCT

There are a lot of responsibilities that come with owning a canine guardian. In this litigious society, it is not desirable to own a dog that bites, runs at large, or disturbs the neighbors. Regardless of the breed of dog you own, it is crucial for you to manage your dog's behavior with obedience training, socialization, and lifestyle management.

OBEDIENCE TRAINING: Obedience training does more than teach your dog how to behave; it also helps you build a strong bond with your dog. Training, when done right, should develop trust and respect between you and your dog. The strength of your relationship with your dog inspires your canine consort to protect you in the first place, so don't neglect to spend as much time training your dog as possible.

Although it's quite possible to train your dog at home if you are skilled in training techniques, there are notable benefits to enrolling in an obedience class. Training classes can provide a novel environment in which to train your dog, since you do not want your dog to learn to be

FAST FACT

Breeds that make good guard dogs include:
- Akita
- American Bulldog
- American Staffordshire Terrier
- Belgian Malinois
- Belgian Tervuren
- Bouvier des Flandres
- Boxer
- Bull Mastiff
- Chow Chow
- Doberman Pinscher
- Dutch Shepherd
- German Shepherd
- Giant Schnauzer
- Great Dane
- Mastiff
- Rottweiler
- Standard Schnauzer

obedient only in his home territory. Group classes can give your dog the opportunity to learn how to behave in the presence of other dogs, and a training instructor can offer expert guidance on training techniques and problem behaviors.

In most areas, you'll find an abundance of dog training classes, but that doesn't mean they are all identical. Scrutinize various training instructors to choose the right one for you and your dog. Although many modern dog trainers now use food rewards quite heavily in their training programs, this type of training model is not always the best for strong-willed guard dog breeds. For this type of dog, a nonfood training program that focuses on effective canine leadership may be better.

Any type of training program you choose should use positive training methods that do not include physical punishment: Harsh or punitive methods tend to make dogs fearful or defensive. Controlling a dog is a mental exercise, not a physical exercise. A good training instructor who has experience with your breed of dog can teach you how to play this "mind game" correctly so that you can achieve control over your dog's behavior.

AKC CANINE GOOD CITIZEN CERTIFICATE: The AKC Canine Good Citizen (CGC) certificate is a worthwhile goal for any dog owner who wants a reliable, well-behaved watchdog or guard dog. This program consists of a 10-part test that evaluates dogs on skills that every good canine citizen should have. Some of these skills include greeting a stranger, walking in a crowd, reacting to other dogs, and coming when called. It also evaluates the care and handling owners give to their dogs.

Many states throughout the country have recognized the value of the CGC program and have adopted resolutions praising it. It has become a part of the testing requirements for

Food treats, accompanied by praise are a great way to reward desirable behavior.

As part of the socialization process, take your puppy for regular walks and introduce him to friendly people that you encounter.

come into social contact with many different people, animals, and environments. Socialization is especially important for young dogs, as they are just beginning to register their impressions and develop their belief systems. Puppies between the ages of 6 and 12 weeks go through a fear development stage that may make them fearful of things they've never been exposed to. So it's crucial to allow young dogs to explore the people and animals in their world, and to make sure their experiences and interactions are positive.

The one thing many people tend to forget about socialization is that it is a lifelong learning process. Socializing a puppy at a young age does not complete the socialization process. Protection dogs need to interact socially throughout their lives, because they have a greater tendency to become overly protective if they live a reclusive lifestyle.

Take your dog for regular walks and make time to talk to your neighbors along the way. Dog training classes and participation in dog sports provide many socialization opportunities for dogs. Playdates with children and other dogs, under adequate supervision, can teach your dog to be comfortable in the company of others. Taking your dog with you to the pet store or when traveling

certified therapy dogs as well. You can get more information on this program by visiting the AKC website, www.AKC.org.

SOCIALIZATION FOR PERSONAL PROTECTION: Socialization helps to shape a dog's perception of the world. In order to develop healthy perceptions, it's vital for a dog to can significantly broaden your dog's horizons. In all situations, always be prepared to protect your dog from bad experiences, and your dog will learn to feel safe in the world.

CONTROLLING BARKING: Your dog's voice is his alarm bell. Some dogs are better at ringing their bells than others. If your dog is a good watchdog, he is sensitive to noises and immediately investigates any little bump in the night. Of course, you want to know when a stranger is encroaching on your property, but you don't need to know about every dead leaf that blows across the lawn. This is where some watchdogs run into trouble.

Good watchdogs have shrill voices and they like to use them, but

when a dog repeatedly gives false warnings or, worse, doesn't know when to stop sounding the alarm, it can be downright annoying. Dogs are born with the right equipment to do the job, but that doesn't mean they know how to use that equipment in the best way. If this is the case with your dog, it's up to you to fine-tune your canine alarm system.

Teach your dog to be a good watchdog by getting up to investigate every time your dog barks. If your dog is alerting you to something legitimate, such as the arrival of company, a strange dog in the yard, or someone vandalizing your vehicle, acknowledge your dog with praise for doing a good job. If it is a harmless "threat," such as a dog on a

A dog that barks constantly without a good reason is a nuisance to the neighbors. The best way to teach your dog not to bark is to train him to "talk," or bark on command, and to stop barking when you tell him "quiet."

FAST FACT

Most of the dogs that win awards for protecting or saving people, such as the Ken-L Ration Dog Hero of the Year Award and the American Humane Association Hero Dog Award, are not specifically trained as protectors. They are simply pets whose strong natural instinct to protect those they love prompts them to become canine heroes. Read stories about these pets at www.dogguide.net/24-hero-dog.php.

leash out for a stroll in front of your house, you can praise your dog for alerting you and then tell your dog that everything is OK and to be "quiet." Once your dog has apprised you of the situation and you let him know there is nothing to worry about, he should cease barking. If he doesn't, you may need to insist that he does. If your dog respects you, he will acquiesce to your judgment.

If your dog is barking at "nothing" (maybe he heard the garbage truck coming down the street), or something totally benign, such as someone walking on the sidewalk a block away, use a scolding voice to express your disappointment. Your dog will soon learn that he has an important job to do and that you do not appreciate false alerts. Again, tell

your dog to "quiet" and be persistent in making sure that he does. A well-trained watchdog is a valuable house-mate.

AVOIDING INAPPROPRIATE AGGRESSION

Protection is a valuable service that dogs provide, but when a dog's protective instinct goes haywire, it produces inappropriate aggression. You can avoid this dangerous behavior problem by practicing effective canine leadership, eliminating risk factors that contribute to inappropriate aggression, and seeking professional help when needed.

CANINE LEADERSHIP: Dogs that have an independent, dominant, or protective nature require firm canine leadership. Without it, they will assume the leadership position for themselves and address situations on their own terms, sometimes with their teeth. A dog that respects his owner as the "pack leader," on the other hand, will defer to the one in control. He doesn't feel a need to take things into his own paws (or teeth) when there is someone more worthy to handle such things.

So how do you become an effective leader that your dog will respect? First, you need to be consistent. You need to be consistent in enforcing

Good early training is very important, because it will give your dog a solid foundation for future learning. Effective training is all about maintaining the top position in the household and being consistent about the rules that you set and how they are enforced.

rules. You need to be consistent in how you communicate with your dog and not use different words to mean the same thing. You need to be consistent in your dog's eating, sleeping, and exercise schedules. Consistency provides security and stability for a dog, and dogs view consistent owners as trustworthy and respect-worthy.

Second, you need to be confident and assertive. Don't take "no" for an answer. Insist on having your own way and don't allow your dog to "win" the battles you choose to fight. It might be easier to just give in to your dog sometimes, but your dog will respect you much more if you are persistent and determined to be the one in control.

Third, you need to be fair to your dog. Don't blame or punish your dog for doing things that come naturally

to dogs. If your dog purposely disobeys because he is abiding by his own will instead of yours, discipline your dog fairly and consistently. Discipline should always consist of the lowest-strength consequence necessary to achieve results, and it should be appropriate for your dog's personality.

Finally, canine leadership requires loads of patience. Your dog will respect you if you are patient with him, when you always give him the benefit of the doubt, and when you remain calm. Dogs view anger as a sign of emotional instability and have difficulty respecting humans who can't control their tempers.

REMOVING RISK FACTORS: There are a number of risk factors that will increase the chance that a dog will engage in unwanted aggression. The following suggestions will help you reduce the likelihood that your dog will bite inappropriately:

- Do not leave your dog chained outside. According to a study by the Centers for Disease Control and Prevention, chained dogs are nearly three times as likely to attack a human as dogs who are not tethered. Another CDC study indicated that chained dogs are involved in more than 25 percent of all dog attacks resulting in a person's death.
- Socialize your dog so that he can develop good social skills with people and other animals.

- Train your dog in basic obedience, so that you can exercise better control over his behavior.
- Have your dog neutered or spayed. Nonsterilized dogs are three times more likely to bite than sterilized dogs, and males are more likely to bite than females.
- Provide constant supervision when outdoors and any time children are present.
- Give your dog a "safe zone" where he can retreat from children. Use door gates, if necessary, to separate your dog from children.
- Educate children in the proper treatment of dogs. Never allow a child to pull on, climb

Dogs that are chained or tethered for long periods of time tend to become highly aggressive. Because such dogs are unable to flee from a threat, whether real or perceived, they are more likely to attack any unfamiliar animal or person who wanders onto their territory.

on, or otherwise treat your dog inappropriately, no matter how tolerant your dog appears to be.

- Protect your dog from potentially harmful situations. Do not be afraid to step in and remove your dog from a situation that may escalate into a dog bite, such as an interaction with a hostile dog.
- Do not leave your dog unattended in a vehicle with the windows cracked open—you never know if someone will try to stick a hand into the vehicle, and your dog may be quite protective of his vehicle territory. It is best to leave your dog at home if you cannot stay with him in the vehicle.

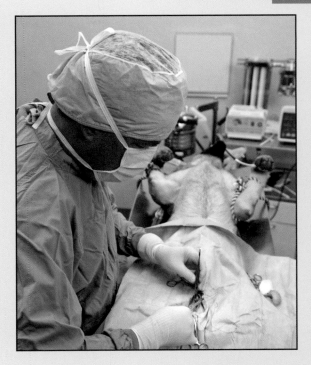

Neutering male dogs eliminates some undesirable sex-related behaviors, such as aggressiveness or marking territory with urine.

SEEKING PROFESSIONAL HELP: If your dog engages in aggressive behavior that you cannot control on your own, do not hesitate to seek the guidance of a professional. There are many different forms of canine aggression, including food aggression, fear aggression, and dominance aggression, and each requires different methods to resolve them. No matter what type of aggression is at the root of your dog's hostility, dog bites are nothing to fool around with.

Seek out a professional canine behaviorist who specializes in aggression issues. A local humane society may have a canine behaviorist on staff who can help you. Ask your veterinarian for recommendations. A list of certified animal behaviorists is also available on the International Animal Behavior Consultants website, www.iaabc.org.

RESPONSIBLE DOG OWNERSHIP

Controlling your dog's protective behaviors is an important part of being a responsible dog owner, but there are many other responsibilities that come with dog ownership, regardless of the type of dog you own. It is in everybody's best interest for dog owners to abide by the laws and expectations of their communities. Such rules exist for the purpose of keeping people and dogs happy and safe when they live side by side.

IDENTIFICATION: One of the best steps you can take to protect your dog is to provide him with a form of identification. Dogs become lost for

A sturdy collar with appropriate ID tags and licenses is a must for your dog.

all kinds of reasons—the dog wanders off, someone accidentally leaves a gate open, or the dog runs off after being frightened by fireworks. Your dog can't tell anyone who he is or where he lives, but identification will ensure that your dog will find his way back home again.

A collar with an ID tag provides an excellent form of readily available identification. Anyone who finds your dog can then easily identify him. Unfortunately, ID tags aren't the most reliable form of ID because collars can fall off or dog thieves may remove them. Experts now recommend that dog owners have their pets microchipped as well.

A microchip is a tiny data capsule that your veterinarian injects under your dog's skin between the shoulders. The microchip is a permanent form of ID that cannot be lost, damaged, or stolen. A scanning device can then detect and retrieve vital information from the microchip if your lost dog finds his way into the hands of a veterinarian or an animal shelter.

LICENSING: Obtaining a license for your dog is another way to help keep your dog safe and to abide by community expectations. Most communities have dog licensing requirements that help them keep track of and control the population of dogs in the community. Such a requirement can help a community enforce a "per household" limit for dogs. This kind of law is put into effect because too many dogs in one location can cause noise and odor that disturbs other residents.

Licensing also allows the community to enforce rabies vaccination requirements. Rabies is a virus that attacks the dog's nervous system and causes horrific symptoms that include unprovoked aggression and the inability to swallow. Since dogs can transmit rabies to humans, and the consequences are most often fatal, controlling the spread of rabies is a very important function of dog licensing.

Supplying your dog with a license tag can also add a little more assurance that your dog will be able to find his way home if he becomes lost. This is clearly a worthwhile benefit of licensing, but the greatest benefit may be how it affects your wallet. Licensing fees are very inexpensive compared to the fines you may have to pay for noncompliance with licensing laws. The best deal is to license your dog as soon as possible after you acquire him.

RABIES VACCINATION: In order to obtain a license, you'll have to prove that your dog has received a rabies vaccination. Your veterinarian will issue a certificate of rabies vaccination that you can supply for this purpose. Thanks to extremely strict rabies vaccination requirements throughout the country, the transmission of rabies from dogs to humans is now basically nonexistent in the United States. But this doesn't mean we can let our guard down and become lax about enforcement. The rate of dog-to-human rabies transmission is still a viable threat in

When it comes to scheduling vaccinations, follow the guidance of your veterinarian.

many underdeveloped countries, and it wouldn't take long for cases in the United States to increase in the absence of strict safeguards.

Most states now require a three-year rabies vaccine, but your veterinarian can advise you as to the exact requirements for your state of residence. Keep your dog's rabies vaccination certificate in a safe place, since you may need to provide it when you register for dog training classes or participate in other activities with your canine friend.

LEGAL LIABILITY: As a dog owner, you are liable for anything your dog does. Certainly, if your dog bites an innocent person, your dog is not the only one who will face consequences—you will, too. But biting someone is not the only kind of trouble that a dog can get into. Your dog may dig up a neighbor's garden, harass a neighbor's cat, or scare a neighbor's children. Any time your dog injures someone or causes property damage, a lawsuit may cost you tens of thousands of dollars.

You can minimize your liability exposure by training your dog and taking precautions to keep your dog under control. Take care to keep your dog confined to your property when he's outdoors and keep your dog on a leash when he's out in public. Provide adequate supervision for your dog to avoid problems. It is also a good idea to carry liability insurance through a homeowner's or renter's insurance policy.

There may be specific laws in

A warning sign is essential if you have a security dog, as it can help to prevent bites on your property.

your community that encourage people to control their dogs. Leash laws may require you to keep your dog on a leash when in public, and nuisance laws may apply to your dog's barking or other nuisance behaviors. Violations can result in fines or other consequences, so take the time to teach your "alarm dog" the "quiet" command, and manage your dog so that he doesn't infringe on the rights of others. This way, your neighbors can value your canine as a good citizen rather than complaining about him.

THE GOOD NEIGHBOR POLICY:

There's more to being a responsible pet owner than abiding by laws. You need to be a good neighbor, and this means being respectful of others in everything you do. Your canine guardian may be a potential hero, but don't expect everyone else to recognize and appreciate his heroic qualities. Some people aren't fond of dogs. Some people are allergic to dogs. And some people are afraid of dogs. For these reasons, you should never allow your dog to approach someone without that person's permission. Practice good manners by asking if your dog can greet a new acquaintance.

If your dog leaves a mess in a neighbor's yard, that can cause con-

flict in the neighborhood. Accidents happen when you own a dog, but it's your duty to clean them up whenever they do. Be sure to confine your dog to your yard as he does his business, and take waste bags with you whenever your dog accompanies you off your property.

There are always positive effects in practicing responsible pet ownership, but the greatest one is this: When you set a good example, others are sure to follow suit. Responsible dog owners help to open more doors for our canine friends. As dogs become accepted in more places, it provides more opportunities to spend time with and enjoy our canine companions. In other words, it makes it a better world for humans and canines alike.

❧❧❧

Regardless of the strength of your dog's natural protective abilities, any dog is better than no dog when it comes to home security. Training and managing your dog in ways that allow you to gain the most benefit from your dog's security services can give you one more reason to enjoy dog ownership. Your dog—no matter how large or small, aloof or friendly, independent or dependent—may become a lifesaver some day.

Organizations to Contact

American Kennel Club (AKC)
260 Madison Ave.
New York, NY 10016
Phone: 212-696-8200
Website: www.akc.org

**American Rescue
Dog Association (ARDA)**
P.O. Box 613
Bristow, VA 20136
Phone: 888-775-8871
E-mail: information@ardainc.org
Website: www.ardainc.org

**American Working Dog
Federation (AWDF)**
Michelle Testa, Secretary
P.O. Box 25
Palmyra, VA 22955
Phone: 434-591-4552
E-mail: michelle@myrivercottage.com
Website: www.awdf.net

**Association of
Pet Dog Trainers (APDT)**
5096 Sand Road SE
Iowa City, IA 52240-8217
Phone: 1-800-PET-DOGS
E-mail: information@apdt.com
Website: www.apdt.com

Canadian Kennel Club (CKC)
89 Skyway Ave., Suite 100
Etobicoke, Ontario M9W 6R4
Canada
Phone: 416-675-5511
E-mail: information@ckc.ca
Website: www.ckc.ca

**DVG America
(Schutzhund Training)**
Sandi Purdi, Secretary
2101 S. Westmoreland Road
Red Oak, TX 75154
Phone: 972-617-2988
E-mail: sandidvg@att.net
Website: www.dvgamerica.com

**International Police
Work Dog Association**
P.O. Box 7455
Greenwood, IN 46143
E-mail: ipwda1@yahoo.com
Website: www.ipwda.org

Kennel Club of the U.K.
1 Clarges Street
London W1J 8AB
United Kingdom
Phone: 0870 606 6750
Website: www.the-kennel-club.org.uk

**National Association
for Search and Rescue (NASAR)**
P.O. Box 232020
Centreville, VA 20120-2020
Phone: 703-222-6277
E-mail: info@nasar.org
Website: www.nasar.org

**National Disaster
Search Dog Foundation**
501 E. Ojai Ave.
Ajai, CA 93023
Phone: 888-459-4376
Fax: 805-640-1848
E-mail: rescue@ndsdf.org
Website: www.searchdogfoundation.org

**National Narcotics Detector
Dog Association**
379 CR 105
Carthage, TX 75633
Phone: 888-289-0070
E-mail: thenndda@yahoo.com
Website: www.nndda.org

**National Police Canine
Association**
P.O. Box 538
Waddell, AZ 85355
Phone: 877-362-1219
E-mail: info@npca.net
Website: www.npca.net

**North American Police
Work Dog Association**
4222 Manchester Ave.
Perry, OH 44081
Phone: 440-259-3169
Fax: 440-259-3170
Website: www.napwda.com

**North American Search Dog
Network (NASDN)**
John Beck, President
10100 Holdrege St.
Lincoln, NE 68527
E-mail: jb30343@windstream.net
Website: www.nasdn.org

**United States Police Canine
Association**
P.O. Box 80
Springboro, OH 45066
Phone: 837-751-6469
Website: uspcak9.com

Further Reading

American Rescue Dog Association. *Search and Rescue Dogs: Training the K-9 Hero*. New York: Howell Book House, 2002.

Balabanov, Ivan, and Karen Duet. *Advanced Schutzhund*. New York: Howell Book House, 1999.

Biniok, Janice. *The Rottweiler*. Pittsburgh: Eldorado Ink, 2010.

Bolan, Sandra. *The Labrador Retriever*. Pittsburgh: Eldorado Ink, 2008.

Hautmann, Chad. *The Boxer*. Pittsburgh: Eldorado Ink, 2008.

Johnson, Glen R. *Tracking Dog: Theory & Methods*, rev. ed. Mechanicsburg, P.: Barkleigh Productions, 2003.

Kopelman, Jay. *From Baghdad with Love: A Marine, the War, and a Dog Named Lava*. Guilford, Conn.: Lyons Press, 2008.

Morn, September B. *The German Shepherd*. Pittsburgh: Eldorado Ink, 2008.

———. *The Golden Retriever*. Pittsburgh: Eldorado Ink, 2008.

———. *The Doberman Pinscher*. Pittsburgh: Eldorado Ink, 2011.

Presnall, Ed. *Mastering Variable Surface Tracking*. Wenatchee, Wash.: Dogwise Publishing, 2004.

Schweitzer, Karen. *The Beagle*. Pittsburgh: Eldorado Ink, 2010.

Internet Resources

www.dogbreedinfo.com

Visit the Dog Breed Info Center website for more information on your favorite breed of security dog.

www.dogplay.com

Do you need to find a "hobby" for your working dog? This site is a great source of ideas for games, sports, and other activities to engage in with your dog.

www.petfinder.com

This website can help you find adoptable dogs through shelters and rescue groups in your area.

www.protectiondogs.com

Canine Protection International offers excellent videos on its website that demonstrate some of the skills and advanced fighting techniques personal protection dogs can learn.

www.uwsp.edu/psych/dog/dog.htm

Dr. P's Dog Training web page provides links to dozens of training articles, many of which are written by experts in their field. Do you need help with a problem behavior? You can find the answer here.

Index

Numbers in ***bold italics*** refer to captions.

Contributors

JANICE BINIOK has written numerous articles and books on companion animals, including *The Rottweiler* (2010), *Adopting a Pet* (2011), and several other volumes in the OUR BEST FRIENDS series. She holds an English degree from the University of Wisconsin–Milwaukee and is a member of the Dog Writers Association of America. Janice lives on a small farm in Waukesha, Wisconsin, with her husband, two sons, and several furry family members. Visit her website at www.TheAnimalPen.com for more information.

Senior Consulting Editor **GARY KORSGAARD, DVM,** has had a long and distinguished career in veterinary medicine. After graduating from The Ohio State University's College of Veterinary Medicine in 1963, he spent two years as a captain in the Veterinary Corps of the U.S. Army. During that time he attended the Walter Reed Army Institute of Research and became Chief of the Veterinary Division for the Sixth Army Medical Laboratory at the Presidio, San Francisco.

In 1968 Dr. Korsgaard founded the Monte Vista Veterinary Hospital in Concord, California, where he practiced for 32 years as a small animal veterinarian. He is a past president of the Contra Costa Veterinary Association, and was one of the founding members of the Contra Costa Veterinary Emergency Clinic, serving as president and board member of that hospital for nearly 30 years.

Dr. Korsgaard retired in 2000. He enjoys golf, hiking, international travel, and spending time with his wife Susan and their three children and four grandchildren.